LADIES IN DISTRESS

By the Same Author

Continued Next Week
World of Laughter
Kops and Custards
Bound and Gagged
Clown Princes and Court Jesters
Collecting Classic Films
Winners of the West
Dreams for Sale

LADIES IN DISTRESS

Kalton C. Lahue

South Brunswick and New York: A. S. Barnes and Company
London: Thomas Yoseloff Ltd

Library of Congress Catalogue Card Number: 72-124207

A. S. Barnes and Co., Inc.
Cranbury, New Jersey 08512

Thomas Yoseloff Ltd
108 New Bond Street
London W1Y OQX, England

ISBN 0-498-07634-2
Printed in the United States of America

To JULANNE JOHNSTON: wherever you are, you're not forgotten.

CONTENTS

INTRODUCTION

As the 20th century began to unfold, the American motion picture was in its infancy. Most of the subjects captured on film had been vignettes from real life, and fictional stories had rarely found their way to the screen, except in the magical curiosities produced by Méliès in France that were imported by enterprising distributors in this country. Fiction was not to become a useful adjunct to the motion picture's success until sufficient techniques were developed to adequately employ it and even Edwin S. Porter's *The Life of an American Fireman* (1902) must be considered as an early documentary. But with *The Great Train Robbery* in 1903, Porter introduced the use of a fictional story line; he even crammed a few simple subplots into the single reel and the movies came to life. While Porter was not the first to attempt this, his effort was by far the most successful and historians have found *The Great Train Robbery* to be a convenient starting point.

For the next decade, the pioneer producers concentrated on story development without identifying cast members to the public, but concurrently, a star system was being created by the very popularity of certain players. During this decade producers learned the value of the screen heroine, and the emphasis on feminine roles reached its apex with the appearance of the first serials in 1913–14, which featured the heroine who could take care of herself. By the time of World War I, motion pictures had become big business, and type casting of players had proven to be a most profitable arrangement by the production companies.

An actor or actress who found financial success in a particular type of role was immediately rushed into another similar picture—Theda Bara is an outstanding example. This did not lead to art, but box-office receipts were considered more important and the system lasted for many decades. Fans came to expect their favorites in a certain mold or image and producers gave it to them in huge quantities. Some actresses were versatile (or fortunate) enough to escape or minimize the effects of typecasting, but most of the super stars owed their success to a certain kind of performance which audiences identified with them and to step out of character often proved unwise.

For those upon whom audiences bestowed universal acclaim, the rewards were great. Weekly salaries running into five figures were possible and the aura of glamor that grew up about the movie star was a heady atmosphere which many were unable to handle. But the homage America paid to its screen favorites in the twenties is not likely to appear again, and while it is sometimes difficult to understand and appreciate the immense amount of devotion which a particular actress evoked, let there be no mistake about it—a movie star in that era was A MOVIE STAR and she lived the image to the hilt.

The aficionado of the silent screen can easily name his particular favorites and while they may not be in complete accord with the forty screen heroines presented within the following pages, I selected those included on the premise that they best represent the many and divergent talents which made the silent days such a pleasant memory for those who were devoted to the darkened movie palaces of so long ago. If I have left out a particular favorite of yours, please bear with me—it does not mean that I think her unimportant, but only that space limitations preclude attempting to satisfy everyone.

My thanks to the many film collectors and individuals who made this volume possible and special thanks for the unusual illustrations should be given the Academy of Motion Picture Arts and Sciences, Larry Edmunds Bookstore, John Hampton's Silent Movie Theatre and the National Film Archives, British Film Institute, who assisted in my attempt to assemble illustrations which are representative of each actress while avoiding those commonly in use.

LADIES IN DISTRESS

MARY ASTOR

Beauty contest winner, Academy Award winning actress and successful authoress, Mary Astor has lived a long and full life, one sufficiently interesting to fill several of her books. Born Lucille Langhanke, the daughter of a music instructor in the midwest, the quiet and retiring little girl's earliest memories were of constantly being pushed by her father to achieve a success he had never known. While still in high school, Lucille halfheartedly entered a beauty competition sponsored by *Shadowland,* a fan magazine, and finished in second place in the 1920 contest, winning a screen test and an appearance in *The Beggar Maid* (1921), a minor independent production. Her father's fondest dreams now appeared on the verge of coming true and the family moved to New York City to actively push her career.

This brought her into contact with Charles Albin, a commercial photographer whose portfolio of the beautiful young girl helped her to land a six-month contract with Famous Players-Lasky. Now known as Mary Astor, Lucille was on the way to fulfilling her father's ambition and the parental pressure continued as he gave up music to become her business manager. During her contract with Lasky, Mary spent many weeks studying acting techniques and did a bit part with Gareth Hughes and May McAvoy in *Sentimental Tommy.* This ended on the cutting room floor and the contract also ended, with no option exercised. The big break was still to materialize, and in the meantime Mary Astor's screen career was at a standstill.

Through the good graces of Albin, she managed to find work

MARY ASTOR

With Lloyd Hughes in *Forever After,* 1926.

in a series of short subjects produced by Holman Day for Pathé release (*The Brother of the Bear, My Lady O' the Pines*) and a few small roles in feature pictures, holding on until April 1923 when Lasky offered a new contract, this time for a full year at $500 weekly. Leaving for Hollywood, one of her first appearances came in a William de Mille picture and led directly to a role on loan-out to Warners. John Barrymore had seen the 17-year-old girl and thought her perfect for his co-star in *Beau Brummel.* Mary's career began to accelerate after this association, and before long she was featured with Douglas Fairbanks, William Boyd and other top stars of the twenties in pictures like *Success, Don Q, Son of Zorro, The Fighting Coward, Rose of the Golden West* and *Two Arabian Knights,* roles which made her a box-office attraction but which Mary considered to be no better than pulp magazine stories. By the late twenties, Mary Astor was a Fox star, earning $3750 weekly on a 40-week contract.

At this point, Mary's father had lost all perspective and was now an extreme annoyance, both to her and to her studio. Brought

***Two Arabian Knights,* 1927, with William Boyd.**

up with a strong sense of respect for her parents, Mary had tolerated her father's interference in her life for many years, but finally asserted her own independence by marrying director Kenneth Hawkes in the spring of 1928. The marriage lasted but a short 18 months, for Hawkes was killed early in 1930 when his plane crashed off Point Vincente while shooting scenes and scouting locations for a new picture. Sound now had the industry firmly in its grasp, and when Mary went back to work it was to conquer a new medium with a role in Paramount's *Ladies Love Brutes.*

Four years later, Mary Astor and her parents clashed publicly when they sued in an effort to compel her to support them. Although Mary maintained that they had cost her over $500,000 in the past five years, the judge ordered her to pay $100 monthly until the case was tried. Mary's out-of-court settlement moved this family quarrel off the gossip pages, allowing her to continue her career with roles in some of the biggest pictures of the decade, *Red Dust, The Prisoner of Zenda* and *Brigham Young.* In 1941, she was cast opposite Humphrey Bogart in a screen version of Dashiell Hammett's

Montagu Love and Mary in *Rose of the Golden West*, 1927.

Heart to Heart, 1928.

The Maltese Falcon. A much better picture that its budget would have led one to expect, *The Maltese Falcon* won Mary acclaim for her role as heroine-villainess and has become a classic of the detective genre over the years. That same year, she won the Academy Award for best supporting actress in *The Great Lie.*

Her long, distinguished career has since encompassed stage, screen, television and several books, but personally I enjoyed her silent films the most. With a regal bearing and poise beyond her years, Mary's delicate beauty was then at its height; and while I suppose that she was right in considering much of her work in silent pictures to rank with pulp magazine stories, I still find it delightful to watch the young Miss Astor in the arms of Barrymore, a man with whom she was obviously infatuated and an actor who had no peers. It's always interesting to watch the maturation of a gifted actress and Mary's silent roles unfolded a talent she never dreamed she had in those early days when her father continually asked, "Don't you ever want to be somebody?"

THEDA BARA

Theda Bara—the name immediately brings to mind the archtypical siren of the silent screen, that heroine who preyed upon the male of the species as a cat toys with a mouse, enjoying every luscious moment of pleasure from its victim's suffering before closing in for the kill. While this reputation has attached itself to Miss Bara over the years, it is by no means an adequate or complete description of her screen characterizations. Sold to the public as a vamp (or more precisely, a vampire) and entrapped before she had a chance to prove herself in any other role, Theda's misfortune was the massive publicity campaign with which William Fox built her into a screen legend.

Screen stardom was the end of a long journey for the little girl from Cincinnati, if indeed that was her birthplace. Various cinema writers have disagreed on her name: some say she was born Theodosia Goodman in November 1892, the daughter of a Cincinnati tailor; other claim she was Theodosia de Coppett, from a theatrical family; and there are those who combine the two stories. A check of the Cincinnati Bureau of Vital Statistics has so far failed to settle the disagreement, but the registrar cautions that this is not an uncommon situation, as compulsory birth registration was not required by law until 1908.

Whatever her exact background, we do know that she was not born out of wedlock to a French artist and his Arab mistress in the shadows of the Egyptian Sphinx, as the Fox studio publicity suggested, nor was she the leading actress of the Theatre Antoine in Paris. While her screen name proved to be a convenient anagram for "Arab Death" and smacked of the mysterious Middle East, her

THEDA BARA

origins were humble enough; Theda was a contraction of Theodosia and Bara came from a relative's surname. Theda's background was reflected both in her speech and the way in which she carried herself. It took a good deal of studio coaching to effect the stiff, regal bearing she was to exhibit early in her career.

Miss Bara's rapid rise was accidental enough; Frank Powell picked her out of the extra ranks to play the heroine in *A Fool*

***A Fool There Was,* 1915.**

***Romeo and Juliet,* 1916. Harry Hilliard as Romeo.**

There Was, his pot-boiler based on the stage play of the same name. This in turn had its origin in Rudyard Kipling's poem "The Vampire." In William Fox's financial condition the use of a star name was out of the question, but its production and subsequent release proved to be one of the greatest favors ever done the dour mogul in his lengthy career. For the next four years, the earnings of Theda Bara's films virtually supported the Fox studio and its efforts to rival Paramount and Universal; 1915 gross rentals of $3.2 million netted Fox over a half million in profits. Not until Tom Mix's films caught on with the public after World War I was Fox to enjoy another star of her box-office magnitude.

An overnight sensation with the release of *A Fool There Was* in January 1915, Theda Bara romped through forty consecutive films in 36 months as she and the Fox directors cranked out footage continuously. Cleopatra, Salome, Carmen, Juliet, Cigarette, Esmeralda—all famed heroines and portrayed by Theda. Somewhat on the stout side, her staring face liberally coated with makeup which the orthochromatic film emphasized, Miss Bara was usually underclad in gaudy costumes which sought to reveal her physical charms, although in light of today's standards, her wardrobe can only be described as quaint.

The forerunner of Hollywood's symbolic woman of the world, Theda's roles were those of the woman who could never be wife and mother, and who turned instead to desire for solace. Bent on destroying any man with whom she came in contact, Miss Bara put all she had into it. Swathed voluptuously in black silk or satin to offset the bareness of her shoulders and arms, she was the embodiment of sheer evil. A dark cloud of hair encircled her round, sensual face. The exotic, heavy-lidded eyes were emphasized out of proportion and the props included in her publicity stills gave credence to the story that she was an alluring, heartless but coldly passionate woman who lived only for sensual pleasure. Sex as such was never directly brought into the open, as in today's films, but it took an unusually naive audience even at that time to miss the suggestion. The symbolism behind this was hammered home hard from the very beginning and progressively exaggerated until it lost all plausibility. Competition from imitation vamps (Valeska Suratt, Virginia Pearson, Louise Glaum) didn't help matters either.

The majority of her early roles were program pictures in the same vein as *A Fool There Was;* the same old story with a change of name, costume and locale. In that now-classic picture, Theda

***Carmen,* 1915**

played The Vampire, a woman of notorious reputation who was inadvertently offended by the wife of John Schuyler, a happily married man. Vowing revenge upon the wife, Theda seduced Schuyler who promptly moved into her quarters and lost all interest in life except for his new lady friend. Knowing her husband was on the road to ruin, the wife begged him to return, and coming to his

***Cleopatra,* 1917.**

senses momentarily he started to return home, only to fall into delirium and drop dead.

Released monthly for three years, Miss Bara's pictures quickly wore the formula to death and although she did other dramatic parts besides the siren bit, it was too late. By the time *Kathleen Mavourneen* appeared on the screen, it was impossible for audiences to accept Theda as an innocent Irish peasant girl. Her performance

***When Men Desire,* 1919.**

was praised by reviewers, who treated Miss Bara kindly, reserving their criticism for the Fox organization for not using better judgment in presenting its star to the public. Actually, many of her portrayals received fine reviews, crediting the actress with rising above the material with which she had been given to work. But Theda Bara had been typecast at the outset of her career as the femme fatale, that supposedly irresistible half-human who set a

***When Men Desire,* 1919. With G. Raymond Nye and Fleming Ward.**

trap for unsuspecting men, attempting to destroy them with her wanton wiles for reasons (as the subtitles told us) "she never knew why and did not understand," only to be foiled at the last moment by outside forces. Theda's films had enough trouble with the censors; no other ending would have slipped by the scissors.

As her career progressed it seemed to require more and more reels to tell the same sordid story, but by 1919 Theda's star had dimmed considerably. Because of other unsuccessful ventures, Fox was losing money and desperate; Bara had a breakdown and could no longer carry the entire studio on her box-office earnings. Theda's salary had risen from $75 a week in 1914 to $4000 in 1918; the cost of producing her films, once made on a shoestring budget, now exceeded $60,000. Fox let her contract expire and turned his once-super star loose.

Bewildered, she tried the stage without much success and then married director Charles J. Brabin in 1921. Another Broadway fling and more personal appearances followed, but nothing seemed to work. Theda Bara Productions was incorporated in 1924 in an effort to restore the queen to her throne, but it never made a film.

In 1925, Theda tried a comeback in Chadwick's *Unchastened Woman,* plus more personal appearances and stage tours. Closing out her career with a few comedies for Hal Roach which burlesqued her vamp characterization, Miss Bara retired to the role of wife and mother so long denied her on the screen. Although accepting the inevitable after a fashion, she never quite understood what had torpedoed her career so quickly and permanently, but it sometimes seemed that Theda was a naive and willing victim of her own publicity instead of the woman of the world she was supposed to be; during the height of her popularity, she once announced with a straight face that her greatest inspirations for playing vamp roles came to her while enjoying a good hot bath. In April 1955, she succumbed to stomach cancer, long forgotten by the public she had once enthralled.

The failure to preserve Theda Bara's vast cinematic efforts constitutes one of the industry's most blatant stupidities; with the exception of her first feature, a few assorted clips and one Hal Roach

***A Woman There Was,* 1919. Robert Elliot.**

The Light, **1919. Eugene Ormonde.**

The Unchastened Woman, **1925. Theda's final feature film.**

***Madam Mystery*, 1926, a Hal Roach two-reel comedy with Jimmy Finlayson (r).**

comedy, her numerous portrayals have been lost. While mention of her name in the past has often elicited chuckles from film critics and historians, her box-office reception strengthens the suspicion that she must have been more than just a passing personality and the available footage, while not completely representative of her career, strongly suggests that Theda had ability beyond a slinky walk and the languid appearance characteristic of existing production stills. But regardless of her talent, to a nation dominated by the rural life and small town morality of the pre-World War I era, Theda's appearance on the screen had been something of a sensation, to put it mildly.

BEVERLY BAYNE

It's difficult to imagine a more famous or popular pair of early screen lovers than the legendary Francis X. Bushman and Beverly Bayne. Their names are invariably brought forth whenever the topic of the silent screen is mentioned, yet this romantic duo remains almost totally unknown to movie buffs. Their career together declined rapidly around World War I and neither made very many pictures in the twenties. The majority of their work was done in the 1913–18 period for Essanay (a firm not noted for its preservation of negatives, release prints or production stills) and Metro's Quality Pictures. As a result, very little of the Bushman-Bayne collaboration has survived the passage of time.

Beverly Bayne came to the screen in 1912 in one of those strokes of good fortune so common to the early motion picture. A Minneapolis girl attending school in Chicago, she was noticed by director Henry McRae Webster, who liked what he saw and offered her work at Essanay. The young girl accepted and soon caught the eye of Bushman, the leading male idol of that era. A married man with several children (a secret carefully guarded by the studio, which felt that its general knowledge would ruin his appeal to the fair sex), Bushman was soon costarred with Miss Bayne, and over the course of the next few years the two were romantically linked in the minds of fans, who saw a very special quality in their appearances together. The two made countless short films for Essanay and were the company's financial mainstay until Charlie Chaplin came along in early 1915.

Shortly after, Fred J. Balshofer lured Bushman to his Quality Pictures to work with Marguerite Snow as his leading lady, but

Beverly Bayne in *Romeo and Juliet.* Imperfections in the 1916 picture mar Miss Bayne's lovely features in this reproduction.

after two films, Bushman refused to start another unless his former costar joined him. In a move to pacify their temperamental star, Quality hired Miss Bayne, who arrived at the studio in time to begin work in *Pennington's Choice* and the on-screen sparks continued to fly through several more features and a serial. When Bushman and his wife were divorced, leaving him free to wed Miss

The Great Secret, an 18-episode serial of 1917.

Red, White and Blue Blood, 1918.

With husband Francis X. Bushman.

Bayne (another marriage also closely guarded from their fans), their screen projections became considerably warmer and warmer.

But the Bushman-Bayne style of Ruritanian romance (which gave the actor a chance to wear those smartly tailored uniforms that added so much to his profile) was to suffer an eclipse during The Great War and so did their careers. While Miss Bayne embarked upon a tour of the Keith and Orpheum circuits, her husband also appeared on the stage, but they were back together in 1923 when Bushman formed F.X.B. Pictures to do *Modern Marriage*. Even so, the twenties were lean years on the screen for Miss Bayne; her roles, mostly in Poverty Row pictures with companies like Warners and Truart, had been few and far apart, and she left the business determined to conquer Broadway.

Long divorced from Bushman, who died a few years ago, Miss Bayne lives quietly in retirement in Scottsdale, Arizona, and only occasionally reminisces about the old days. It's a pity that but a small handful remain of the several hundred pictures in which she appeared, making it impossible to properly assess her place among the screen heroines with any degree of fairness. About all we have left is a legend kept alive by the dusty memories of those who saw Miss Bayne perform in her prime a half-century ago, but that is part of the fascination the silent screen holds today for a generation which grew up with television as its babysitter. If nostalgia plays any role at all in the revived interest in the silent movies (and it does), one must certainly place Beverly Bayne high on the list of those whose artistry transcended the silence in which they performed.

CLARA BOW

It's a shame that Clara Bow has become symbolic of the Jazz Age; she wasn't all that wicked or daring, even to the generation that adored her. In fact, most of Clara's films were pretty innocent affairs. Much was hinted at by the suggestive titles (which led you to expect a good deal more than you knew you'd see) but nothing much really took place on the screen, in spite of the suggestive and daring advertising which invariably accompanied each film. After reaching stardom, Clara's roles were usually those of a rather naive young girl who led a hectic life on-screen without understanding it or her own motivations, but who always managed to resolve events for a happy finish.

Clara Bow was a product of her times—a larger-than-life prototype—during an era when the nation's moral code and concept of "the good life" was in rapid flux. Topped with a bob of fluffy red hair, her boyish figure clad in silk stockings and short skirts, Clara smoked and drank to the utter amazement of some and the complete enjoyment of the rest of her fans, who sent her some 20,000 letters weekly at the height of her career. Flaunting sexuality in a representation of the modern girl who had risen above the conventional morality of Main Street, her screen character enjoyed this new-found freedom, and while suggesting the frivolous, promiscuous young woman of the Roaring Twenties, Clara used her pouting femininity to assure herself of an easy life filled with pleasure. It was an image that caught the public's attention, making the attractive Miss Bow a national heroine and allowing Paramount executives to get a good night's sleep for a change, dreaming of the overflowing cash boxes in theaters around the world.

CLARA BOW

***The Plastic Age,* 1925, with Donald Keith.**

Clara's rise to fame was not all that sudden; it had started in 1923 when she was given a role in Elmer Clifton's *Down To The Sea In Ships,* one of the better pictures of that year, and her portrayal showed a marked talent for light and unassuming comedy. A lengthy series of independent pictures for B. P. Schulberg followed, but Clara seemed to flounder in the majority of them. Usually cast as a flapper in a Jazz Age setting, Clara's characters never quite came off, a failing that can only be attributed to the production of her films, which often lacked a solid story or good direction and reflected the lack of money behind them. It almost seemed that no one really knew what to do with her, except to keep grinding out film.

But when Schulberg joined Paramount, he took Clara with him, and as a screen property her value began to rise overnight. Good stories filled with fluff and froth, leading men like Antonio Moreno and Warner Baxter, and the talents of top directors like William Wellman and Herbert Brenon joined forces with Clara's vivacious personality to put her on top. After a sensational appear-

***Kid Boots*, 1926, with Eddie Cantor.**

***Mantrap*, 1926, Ernest Torrence and Percy Marmont.**

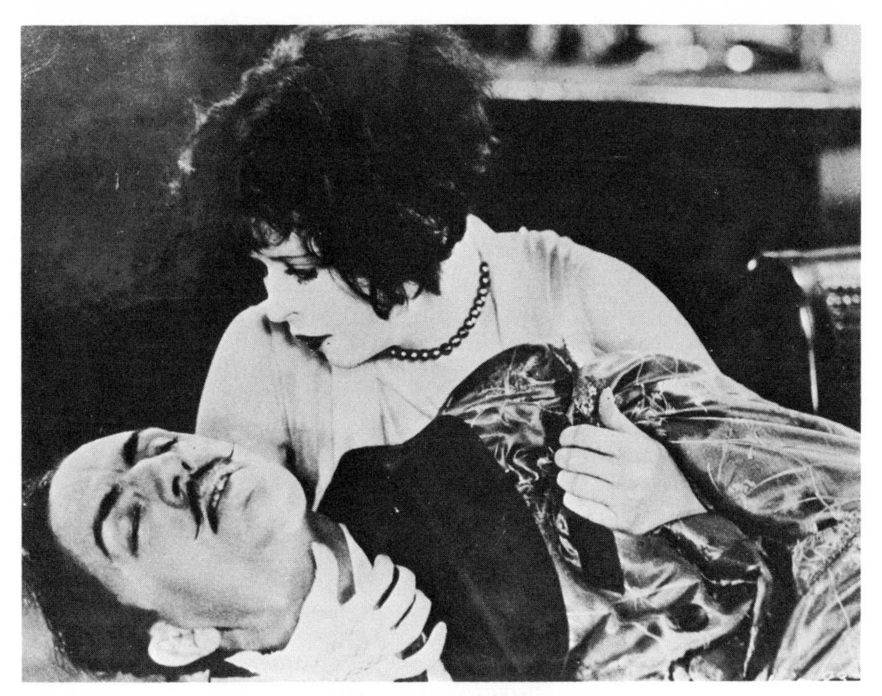

The Runaway, 1926, William Powell.

The *It* Girl, Clara Bow.

***It*, 1927, Antonio Moreno.**

ance as the flapper daughter in *Dancing Mothers* (1926), Clara went on to make the film which gave her stardom but turned out to be probably her worst picture. *It* was taken from the novel by Elinor Glyn and referred, of course, to sex appeal, which the heroine (Clara) possessed in ample quantities. While the resulting film was rather dull and stodgy by Jazz Age standards, *It* and Miss Bow immediately became synonymous, like Valentino and *The Sheik* had a few years before. Although far from a critical success, this one film did more for Clara's career and reputation than any three of her others.

By the time *Wings* came along, Clara managed to stuff herself into a Red Cross uniform long enough to give a memorable performance with Buddy Rogers and Richard Arlen, in spite of the fact that Harold Perry's fine aerial photography stole the picture from the cast. *Wings* also demonstrated that Clara had a talent beyond that of sex appeal, although she was quite possibly one of the most attractive nurses ever to wear the uniform.

Single and living at home, the victim of an unhappy family life, Clara put all she had into the production of her films and what extra energy was left over went into living it up. Clara, her fast convertible and seven red chow dogs became a familiar sight to Hollywood residents, accustomed to even more unorthodox behavior from their celebrities. As the epitome of Flaming Youth, Clara was challenged by other and more durable actresses (Joan Crawford, Louise Brooks, Alice White) but none who captured the public fancy as intensely as had the Brooklyn-born redhead; the nation avidly devoured every scrap of news and rumor about her (even to a public scrap with her secretary Daisy DeBoe) which emanated from the gossip mill and publicity machine called Hollywood.

But Clara's reign (1926–29) was a short one, for an era was about to end, and with it screen glamor took a nosedive into the dregs of reality. The Great Depression climaxed the Roaring Twenties only a few months after sound had established its foothold firmly on the industry and the Clara Bow legend died a quick death.

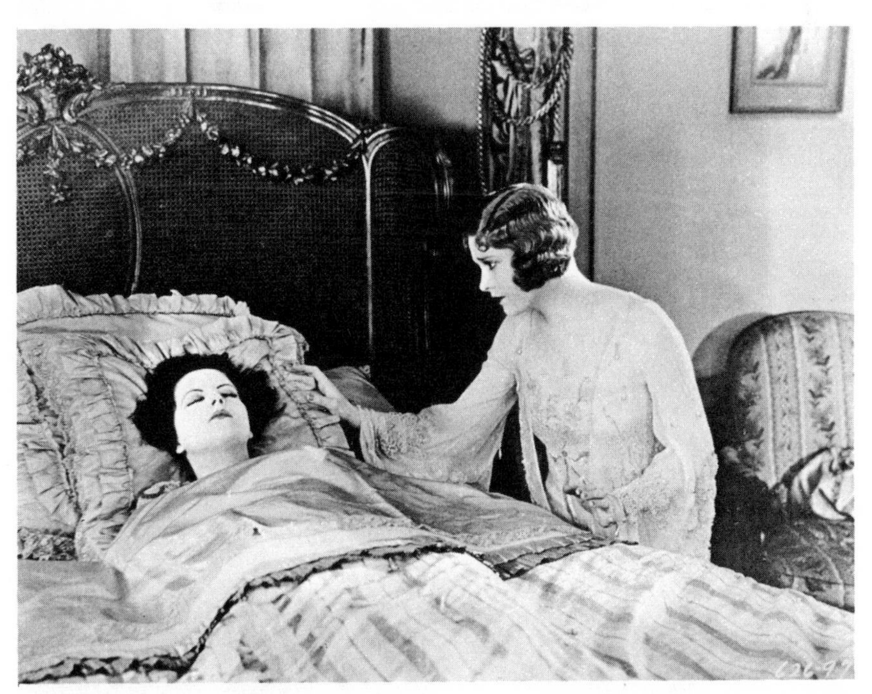

***Children of Divorce,* 1927, Esther Ralston. Miss Ralston's gown for this scene was pink chiffon and embroidered with tiny pearls at a cost of $684.23.**

Hula, **1927, with Clive Brook.**

The Fleet's In, **1928, James Hall.**

***Wings, 1929,* with Buddy Rogers and Richard Arlen.**

A rare moment of ease turned out to be a studio publicity session. Cheesecake and Clara were well acquainted.

Clara made several talkies early in the thirties—films such as *Dangerous Curves,* a circus picture with solid story values and good acting performances from its stars—but the magic was gone and she decided wisely to face her career as her screen character would have—with a happy finish and no tears. With cowboy Rex Bell, she retired from the screen to a ranch in Nevada and enjoyed a marriage which lasted until he died in 1962, marred only by a nervous condition which developed in her later years and required isolation and solitude as prescribed by her doctors. Clara passed away in 1965, but while she had been "The 'It' Girl," she had reigned supreme and although many have tried to imitate her, it's quite improbable that there'll ever be another just like Clara Bow.

LOUISE BROOKS

In recent years, the brief screen career of Louise Brooks has taken on all the trappings of a full-blown cult, especially in Europe. In some respects, Miss Brooks has contributed knowingly or otherwise to its growth. With a candor that's refreshing in a world apparently hell-bent toward hypocrisy, her brilliant articles written for film periodicals in recent years spur on her fans (most of whom are too young to remember her on the screen), who have raised Miss Brooks to the status of a minor legend—an idolatry based almost entirely upon revivals of her pictures at film societies and archives around the world. At the same time, this former star leads the life of a near-recluse in Rochester, New York, rarely seen in public and seldom entertaining visitors.

Beginning professionally at age fifteen under the tutelage of Ruth St. Denis and Ted Shawn, this Cherryvale, Kansas, girl was first and foremost a dancer, moving into George White's *Scandals* and *Café de Paris* in 1924, and then on to Ziegfeld's 1925 *Follies.* A bit role in *The Street of Forgotten Men* that same year brought her to the attention of movie fans, and with a kind of luminescent beauty which defies definition she proved an utterly captivating creature on the giant screen. Her early pictures at Paramount were collegiate types in frothy flapper comedies like *Rolled Stocking* and *The American Venus*, and Paramount, with its usual lack of perception, concentrated almost entirely on presenting her face and figure—commodities much more easily exploited than her talent. This attitude kept Louise tightly reined, preventing her from doing much serious work. By the time *A Girl in Every Port* came along in 1928, trade reviewers could only report that the star was "solid

LOUISE BROOKS

***It's the Old Army Game,* 1926.**

with the jelly bean trade" and *Variety* commented that "little has been said to date about Miss Brooks' acting. It's one of those things you don't mention."

The dramatic ability and talent beneath the bobbed hairdo was overlooked by the power structure again in her outstanding performance with Wallace Beery and Richard Arlen in *Beggers of Life* later that year. An intelligent, perceptive and sensitive actress, Louise was understandably upset about the material with which she was given to work and the restrictive attitudes of the producers and directors who had succumbed to the blandishments of the system, grinding out "safe" pictures in ever-increasing numbers.

But if Louise Brooks's screen career in American films was mismanaged, neglected and sabotaged by the ignorance of the inbred system, she proved her contention in two German films for G. W. Pabst. The mid-twenties had seen the high tide of foreign talent arrive in America, most of whom eventually returned home, disillusioned after tasting the creative inhibitions imposed upon them. But just before the decade ended, the situation reversed itself, with several American stars going abroad to make pictures they wanted to do—pictures with themes that Hollywood would not touch.

As Lulu in *Pandora's Box,* Louise played the mistress who had persuaded her lover to marry, then discovered her attraction for his son was stronger. When her husband found them together, she struck back in anger, killing him. Eventually joining her new and younger lover in poverty, Lulu was forced to take to the streets as a prostitute, falling prey in the end to Jack the Ripper. Ghastly stuff today, it must have been equally as powerful in 1929 (if not more so) and provided Miss Brooks with the opportunity to display those abilities upon which Hollywood would never have gambled.

This picture and *Diary of a Lost Girl* were stark silent drama —psychological sex stories that have contributed heavily to her reputation over the years, especially abroad. Before returning to this country, she made *Beauty Prize* in France, another unusual film which must be counted with the Pabst films among her top performances. Louise never really resumed her career in American films upon her return to this country, partly because of the change-

With Richard Arlen and James Hall in *Rolled Stockings,* 1927.

***Now We're In the Air,* 1927.**

over to sound, but to a great degree her undeniable reluctance to submerge herself in the system once again asserted itself, and after a few uninteresting parts she simply turned her back and walked out, ending her screen career while still in her twenties.

Louise Brooks never fitted into the intellectual and social vacuum that enveloped Hollywood in the twenties; she had too much honesty and self-respect to pay the price success demanded

Victor McLaglen and Louise in *A Girl in Every Port,* 1928.

***Pandora's Box,* 1929.**

of her, and unlike her husband Eddie Sutherland (a comedy director who had learned his trade with Mack Sennett), she was unwilling to practice the deception of self-proclaimed artistry on a day-to-day basis. As a result, Louise was a prominent but never an important star of the silent screen and her reputation today as a serious actress rests mainly upon the work with Pabst.

At this point, an interesting question presents itself—if Louise Brooks had been able to continue with serious dramatic roles in an atmosphere more conducive to creativity, and had she appeared in more than a handful of pictures, would her work have lived up to the legend which surrounds her and her career today? I don't pretend to know the answer and I strongly suspect that Miss Brooks would dismiss the entire topic as being irrelevant and presumptuous, but you must admit, it's a fascinating point for conjecture, especially if you belong to her growing band of admirers.

GRACE CUNARD

As writer, director, actress and sometime film editor, Grace Cunard's many talents graced the early screen in much the same vein that Ida Lupino would strike some 40 years later. Born Harriet Mildred Jefferies in Columbus, Ohio (although later studio publicity set her birthplace in Paris), Grace was a show business veteran at age 17. During the 1910 season she found herself between roles, and hearing that the money was good and the work regular she entered pictures with Biograph. The following year she joined Lubin and then moved to Kay Bee in 1913, where she met Francis Ford, a former actor and make-up artist whose film career had also resulted from a scarcity of stage parts. The two struck up an immediate working friendship which would soon establish both as stars.

A unit director at Kay Bee who chafed under Tom Ince's strong rein, Ford longed to exercise his own ideas free from the dictates of others, and within a few months Grace had convinced him to join Universal with her. By this time, the team had become one of the most prolific in the business. Both had a flair for melodrama and wrote their own scripts, directing and playing the lead roles, then cutting and titling the finished product. From the day they moved to Universal, one was not to be seen on-set or on-screen without the other, and when Ford and Cunard made their (and Universal's) first chapter play, the two became overnight stars.

Although serial fame did not strike Grace with the same force that it had Pearl White, *Lucille Love, Girl of Mystery* was so successful that it committed Carl Laemmle to a serial production program which lasted four decades and made Universal a close

GRACE CUNARD

rival to Pathé during the silent period. Strangely enough, Grace almost refused the part assigned her (which she had not written) in this two-reel western, which was expanded into 15 two-reel episodes. As originally conceived, her role was slight and it appeared to be a waste of her time. But Universal convinced Grace to go ahead, and when *The Perils of Pauline* was released in April 1914, Miss Cunard moved rapidly to meet the challenge. Suggesting that Universal change the title and allow her to expand the story line in other directions, the first Cunard-Ford chapter play took form, with each episode completed just a day or two before release.

Surrounded by the tools of her trade, Grace plots out tomorrow's action.

Having toiled for nearly five years in the movie business without much public acclaim for her efforts, Grace was amazed at the public reaction to *Lucille Love* and soon felt the financial rewards of public adulation. By 1916, she was earning $450 weekly, a rather modest salary, but one supplemented by payment of .25 per foot of finished film (over 1500 feet) in addition to 10 percent of the net profits for her writing-directing, which brought her weekly gross into the four figure bracket.

While appearing together in countless westerns, society dramas and circus pictures (Grace's favorite), Cunard and Ford were often on opposite sides of the law, or pretending to be; the undercover agent or secret service operative was a favorite theme for both. If Grace portrayed the lady cop, Ford turned out to be the master criminal, and then in their next film the two would swap roles. Attractive, but certainly not beautiful, Grace was an action heroine; the kind of girl to whom extraordinary things happened as everyday occurrences. But Miss Cunard was not dependent upon any male to pry her out of a tough spot—this lady proved to be more dan-

In the Fall of '64, one of the Ince films featuring Grace and Francis Ford.

A daring pose from *Dante's Inferno.*

Ford and Cunard's version of the Sepoy Indian Wars, *The Campbells Are Coming.*

Lucille Love, Girl of Mystery

Grace is restrained as the villains pistol whip Eddie Polo in *The Broken Coin.*

Grace as "My Lady Raffles" in *The Mysterious Hand* with Francis Ford.

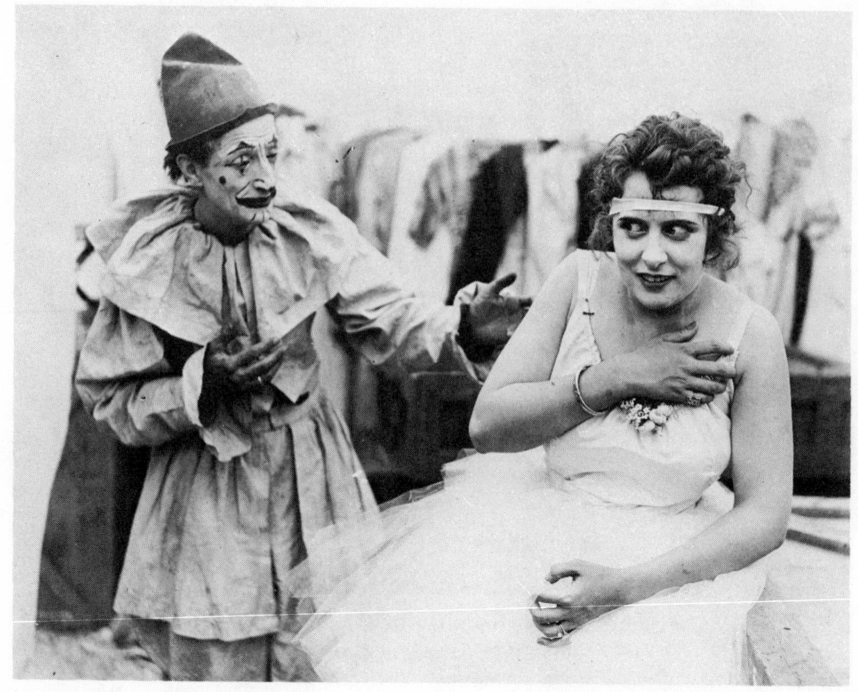

Circus Sal,* with Pete Girard in a make-up he duplicated for a similar role in *The Adventures of Peg O' the Ring.

gerous to her adversaries than nitroglycerin. Tough and single-minded on-screen, Grace usually had her own way, even if it meant unlimbering the petite revolver which found use in a large number of her pictures.

The Cunard formula was a simple but effective one for early screen audiences—establish the characters immediately, plunge into a mystery and incorrectly point the finger of justice once or twice, then close quickly with a surprise ending. This was an approach that had long before become a cliché. The important thing, of course, is that it invariably worked, and sufficiently well to bring the fans back for more next week.

Grace reached the peak of her screen fame with *The Purple Mask* (1916). Produced by the Stern Brothers for Universal, it was the fourth and last of the Cunard-Ford serials. By the time filming was completed, Grace had physically worn herself out, working days in front and behind the camera, settling long arguments with the Sterns and then working far into the night at the typewriter, or in the cutting room. The constant pace of producing serial episodes, along with a steady flow of two- and three-reel subjects brought her close to the point of physical and mental exhaustion, and culminated with Universal allowing her contract to expire after the completion of *Elmo, the Mighty* with Elmo Lincoln in 1919. Grace had been scheduled to make *Elmo, the Fearless* next, but was unable to pull herself together and so Louise Lorraine replaced the star, beginning her own serial career which would endear the charming Miss Lorraine to chapter play fans the world over.

In 1920, Grace signed to do a series of short subjects for Marion Kohn Productions, to be released by National Film Corporation. Cole Hebert (Slim Cole) costarred in these two-reel comedy-dramas, but Miss Cunard was eventually forced to leave the screen for a long rest. Marrying stuntman Jack Shannon in 1925 proved to be the best possible medicine and in 1927, Grace reappeared as the mysterious *Woman in White* in Universal's *Blake of Scotland Yard.* Making the transition to sound easily enough, she worked in character roles until 1942, when an old injury dating back to her serial

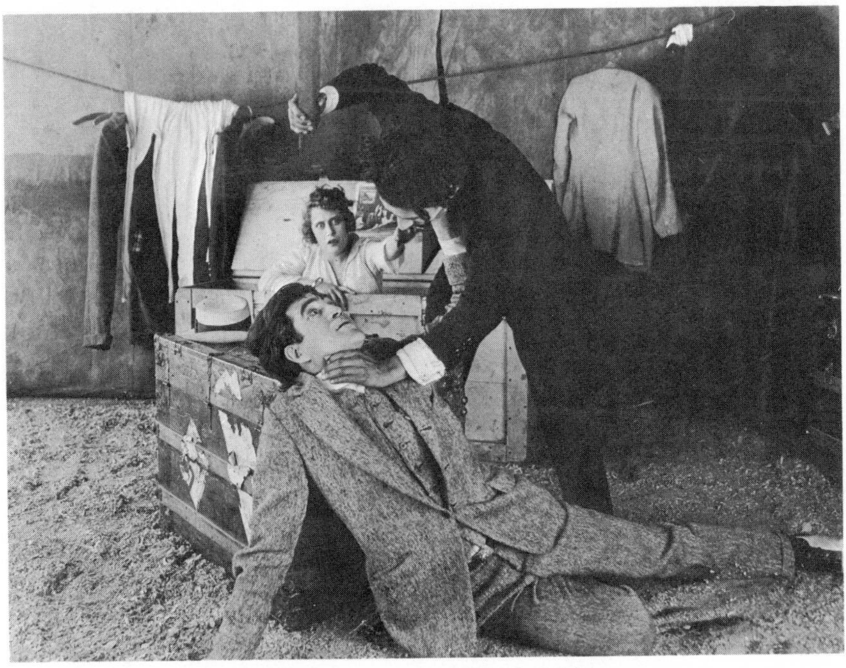

The Adventures of Peg O' the Ring.

As Pat Montez in *The Purple Mask,* Grace was "Queen of The Apaches" and led a band of hooded jewel thieves.

days required a corrective operation. Recovering, Grace returned to work but found the parts fewer and farther between, and in 1945 she retired completely from the business.

During a lengthy career, Grace had found her greatest fame

Grace, as the mysterious "Woman in White" in *Blake of Scotland Yard,* Universal's 1927 cliff hanger.

in the four Cunard-Ford serials of 1914–16. She was also responsible for bringing Eddie Polo to the chapter play screen with a role in *The Broken Coin,* a contribution in itself to serial fans of the 1914–22 period. While her style of rousing melodrama was outdated by the twenties, the grim visage of Miss Cunard staring at

Francis Ford over the barrel of her revolver is one that screen fans old enough to remember have not forgotten.

It's a pity that very little of her work has survived and none is available to the general public today, but shortly after her death in 1967, I spent some time going through the souvenirs of her career with her husband (now deceased) and discovered several dusty reels of 35mm film. A careful examination of these remnants from the past proved to be an intriguing experience. One day, they may be made available for the enjoyment of those who do recall this daring lady of the silent screen, and for the edification of those who would like to know what made the early movie theaters such a fascinating place to spend idle hours. Grace could show them several reasons.

MARION DAVIES

Writing both the script and titles for *Runaway Romany,* Marion Davies made her screen debut in 1918. While appearing in a New York chorus line that same year, she met publisher William Randolph Hearst, who took an immediate and active interest in her and her career. Certain that he had stumbled onto star material, Hearst spent over $7 million in the next decade to make her a leading star. He reorganized the Marion Davies Picture Corporation to form the Cosmopolitan Corporation, producing her films from scripts written by high-priced talent like Frances Marion, whom Hearst paid $2000 weekly to create starring vehicles for his protege.

No aspiring chorus girl could have asked for more, but Marion failed to make the really big splash which Hearst sought. Given the opportunity, Miss Davies might have become a pretty fair comedienne, as she was not exactly without talent. But Hearst saw her only as the symbol of youthful innocence and Marion was forced to argue the point for roles in *The Fair Coed* and *The Patsy,* two of her better light comedies. The man who created her stardom thus circumscribed it to suit his own whims. But those around him, including Marion, were not deluded about her dramatic acting and the fact that she refused to take her pictures seriously annoyed Hearst to no end.

While the subject of Marion's talent (or lack of it) has caused heated debate among film fans, few can deny that she belonged to the royalty of Hollywood and most would agree that she was probably as close to being its Queen as any actress in the twenties. Luxury surround her at work and at play; a 14-room bungalow adorned the front of M-G-M's lot and when Miss Davies left the

MARION DAVIES

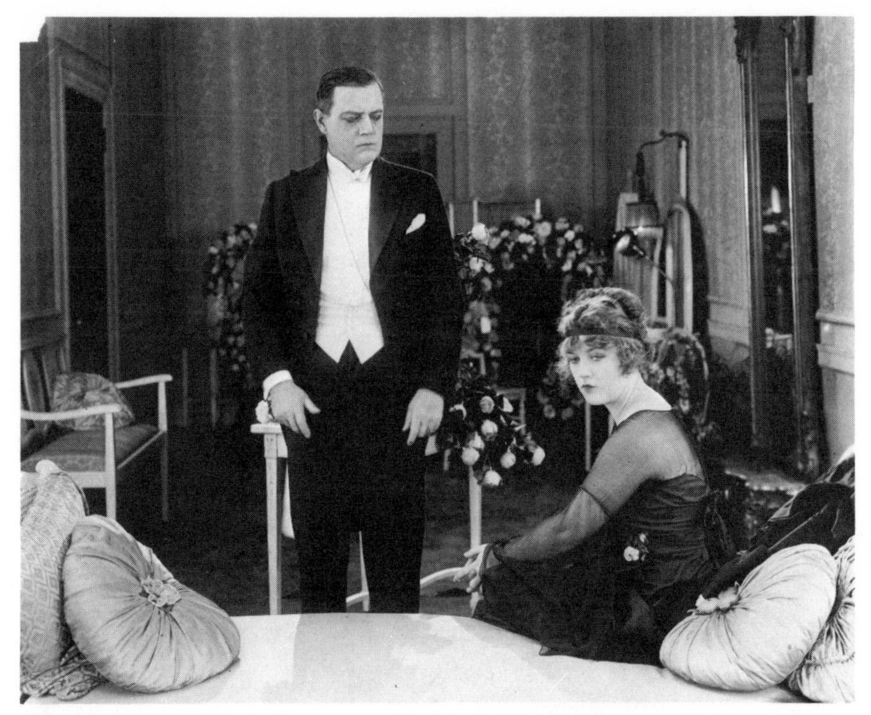

Anders Randolph and Marion in *The Cinema Murder*.

studio after work, she retired either to her Beverly Hills mansion, or to the palatial beach house (110 rooms, 55 baths) in Santa Monica, where she held court on weekends not spent up the California coast at San Simeon, her benefactor's castle-by-the-sea. Not bad for a poor girl, who hosted the liveliest parties in town, invitations to which held a special social significance for the recipients. It was quite a rise in the world for Marion Douras, the daughter of a Brooklyn judge, and she played her role well.

That a newspaper publisher was able to make her a leading screen name (but not a box-office draw) was a tribute to his publishing empire, but in retrospect, for a man whom historians sometimes credit with creating the Spanish-American War, it was probably only an expensive minor feat. A kingmaker, William Randolph Hearst was a man considered by some to be of presidential timbre and he amply rewarded those who cooperated in his many ventures with profuse kind words in print. Those who displeased him were treated by the Hearst papers to the cold shoulder, or even worse,

William Randolph Hearst and Marion at a party held at Hearst's palatial mansion in the mid-twenties.

to a vicious campaign designed to cause as much damage as possible.

Sam Goldwyn saw fit to cooperate by releasing Marion's Cosmopolitan Pictures, and once Goldwyn merged with Metro, Louis

B. Mayer even found it appropriate to completely finance her films with M-G-M's money, giving Hearst a share of the profits. The best of friends with Louella Parsons and Hedda Hopper, in the years before the columnists became disenchanted with each other, Marion was a favored subject of the two most influential gossips who reported on Hollywood, but interestingly enough, several of Marion's pictures received kind treatment in the pages of Hearst's competitors.

Even though many of her films were well-mounted spectaculars, exhibitors resisted Marion's pictures with a determination that once caused an M-G-M salesman to rise at a sales meeting chaired by no less a personage than the venerable Louis B. Mayer to ask why the company forced him to handle such a product. Mayer's lengthy and rambling response failed to provide an answer. Of her many films, *When Knighthood Was in Flower* provided Miss Davies with her best role, but only *Lights of Old Broadway* was

***Buried Treasure*, 1921.**

***When Knighthood Was in Flower,* 1922.**

box-office material sufficient to warrant continued production of the expensive films in which she was starred.

While Marion might not have been a great dramatic actress, she was a superb businesswoman and shrewdly pyramided her earnings (reputed to be $10,000 weekly at the height of her career) into a fortune. When Hearst's empire was on very shaky ground

***Adam and Eva,* 1923.**

With W. C. Fields in *Janice Meredith,* 1925.

Beverly of Graustark, **with Antonio Moreno, 1926.**

in the mid-thirties, it was Marion who came to his rescue with an outright loan of over $1 million to shore up the faltering organization. Hearst repaid this generosity by assigning stock voting rights in her name, and at his death the heirs were astounded to find that control of the entire Hearst empire rested in her hands; she relinquished it for the sum of $1.00 a year.

Not only a hard-headed business woman, Marion also took an active interest in charitable causes at an early age, and in 1924 she established the Marion Davies Foundation Clinic with a $1.2 million grant. Her strong moral and financial support over the years saw the clinic grow into one of the major institutions for child treatment and research in the Los Angeles area. She also sponsored Christmas parties for underprivileged children in New York City for many years.

Marion never married while Hearst was alive, but after his death, she eloped with Horace G. Brown, who preceded his name with an honorary "Captain" from his sea-faring days. Their years

Quality Street, 1927.

The Cardboard Lover, 1928.

Marion at the height of her popularity.

together made interesting headlines approximately twice a year. Brown, whom the press pointed out bore a strong physical resemblance to Miss Davies's former sponsor, enjoyed the role of clown and periodically broke up her parties with his hard-drinking, free-swinging approach to life. After each fracas, the pair would separate publicly and then Marion would relent and take him back after the appropriate public repentance had been made.

Her death in 1961 ended one more colorful chapter of Hollywood history, removing another of those who had helped give the film capital its reputation for glamour in the twenties. Marion's off-screen career was of far more interest to fans than her movies; reams of gossip and speculation have been written about her over the years, yet very little serious evaluation of her acting has been printed. Discussion of Marion Davies usually ends up in one of two firm positions—there was little talent with which to work, or the management of her career was a disaster which robbed the public of her full potential. King Vidor, who enjoyed quite a reputation as a director during her years on the screen, always maintained that Marion was very much underrated as an actress; the real answer will come only when a definitive study of her life and films appears.

PRISCILLA DEAN

When Priscilla Dean made her professional debut on the stage with Joseph Jefferson in *Rip Van Winkle,* she was still an infant. This debut was not a particularly notable feat—as many cute and clever babies have a brief whirl in front of the footlights, growing up to be perfectly normal, well-adjusted spectators. However Priscilla was born into a theatrical family, the daughter of Mary Preston Dean. Traveling with her parents in their small stock company, little Priscilla played a variety of roles as she grew up on the stage—a childhood somewhat removed from that which society at the time considered to be normal.

By the age of 10, the well-versed little actress had won a role with James A. Hearne in his play *The Children of Kings,* and went out on her own. After the play finally closed, she joined the Ben Greet Players, touring the country and adding a variety of Shakespearian roles to her repertoire. When she first encountered motion pictures at age 14, Priscilla had almost the same number of years experience and came highly recommended to Phillips Smalley. He lured her away from the stage momentarily to work in three of his single-reel films.

Working before a live audience was considerably different from emoting in front of the inanimate camera, and once she was finished with Smalley, Priscilla didn't bother to look further for screen work; she returned to the stage where she felt comfortably at home. But paths have a strange way of crossing and while performing her speciality dance in *The Follies Bérgère,* the young Miss Dean came to the attention of D. W. Griffith, whose reputation as a director

PRISCILLA DEAN

at the Biograph studio was growing every day. Griffith liked to boast that he would rather work with a non-professional, a person from whom he could pull a polished performance with ease, and he was captivated by the youthful dancer. Priscilla wasn't interested

With Niles Welch in *Shadows*.

at first, but Griffith put on a stellar performance of his own; when he wanted something badly enough to perform for it, D. W.'s persuasive personality could fire the imagination of the uninitiated with electricity and he wanted to mold Priscilla Dean into a screen star. So it was that Priscilla, captivated by this charming Southerner, capitulated and joined Biograph in 1911.

But Griffith was busy at Biograph and as other problems arose to take his time, interest in his new find soon disappeared. Impatient with the slow progress she was making toward stardom at Biograph, Miss Dean moved to Universal, where work in the comedy and short subject programs was plentiful. Adapting her stage techniques to the silent screen, Priscilla appeared with the comedy team of Lyons and Moran in many of their popular comedies over the next five years, and also found time for numerous appearances in comic dramas like *Somebody Lied.* It was her performance in *The Gray Ghost,* a Universal serial of 1916, which attracted the attention of Lois Weber, who was casting the feature production, *Even As You and I.* Miss Weber gave Priscilla a role in this picture and the result shocked Universal executives when they saw the rushes—here was a potential star on their own lot and no one had noticed her before!

Between 1918 and 1920, Universal carefully groomed Priscilla Dean for stardom, building up her roles in films like *The Brazen Beauty, The Wicked Darling* and *The Exquisite Thief.* She was assigned to director Tod Browning, who began to weave a spell of success around her as he would later do with another seasoned veteran, Lon Chaney, in a series of macabre tales. Browning also adapted many of the stories which they filmed and the pair worked well together. In the summer of 1920, Universal gave him *The Virgin of Stamboul* to direct, and while it was to have been just another program picture Browning cast Priscilla in this melodramatic story of East vs. West and an ill-fated love. Once the front office saw the rough film, they recognized that Priscilla had given a superb performance and decided that this should be released as one of their season's specials. Accordingly, *The Virgin of Stamboul* became a Universal Jewel, scoring heavily with fans and critics alike, receiving heavy play dates and earning a nice return at the

As "Cigarette" in *Under Two Flags* (1922), with James Kirkwood.

***Wild Honey,* with Noah Beery, 1922.**

box-office. As a result, Priscilla was given a series of good stories during 1921–23 (*Outside The Law, Flame of Life, Under Two Flags, White Tiger*), with Browning continuing to direct most of her pictures.

Although she continued making films throughout the silent

Wild Honey **again, this time with Wallace Beery.**

period, Priscilla's career peaked just about 1923. Her best work and greatest popularity came during the association with Browning, for while she worked with Wesley Ruggles and other good directors, Browning alone seemed able to get that little extra snap which made the difference between a good performance and a star por-

Grim determination in a publicity still from *White Tiger,* 1923.

trayal. Once they went their separate ways, Priscilla's stardom gradually faded. Her pictures haven't been revived in many years now. Miss Dean doesn't put too much stock in having been one of the top stars at Universal, but she does admit that it was a

Strong emotion as our heroine faces up to villainous Walter Long.

***The Crimson Runner,* and Alan Hale, 1925.**

What a way to say "Goodnight"!

lot of fun. She still enjoys recalling that golden era a half-century ago when the movies were king of the entertainment world and she was one of the queens.

DELORES DEL RIO

While the silent screen was populated by dozens of women thought to be the world's loveliest in their day, standards of feminine beauty change somewhat from one generation to another; but fortunately those endowed with true beauty have been admired in every age. Although many would still cast their ballot for Greta Garbo as the screen's most desirable heroine in the twenties, I'll throw mine at the feet of Delores del Rio every time. There is no doubt that Garbo's features held a fascination which grew into a legend, but for sheer classical perfection, Miss del Rio deserves her own fan club. She was most every man's dream of a fiery Latin sunset; a strong-willed feminine challenge waiting to be tamed; a shimmering moonbeam of perfection. In all fairness, I may be a bit carried away with Delores, but can you blame me?

There have never been doubts about her acting abilities; from the tender *Ramona* and the tempestuous *Loves of Carmen* to the compassionate Indian mother of *Cheyenne Autumn* a few years back, Miss del Rio has shown a strength and versatility seldom matched in a career spanning both the silent and sound eras, lasting well over four decades and encompassing two nations. While Delores had a number of really choice roles in the waning days of the silent screen, it was her misfortune to appear too late in the period to make a profound impact. Unlike Garbo, whose enigmatic personality lent itself perfectly to the press-agent's dream of an embryonic legend, Miss del Rio's warm, outgoing manner did not harbor the seed of mystery, but her eyes did contain a sparkling fascination for many of us—one which surely could have melted an iceberg had she ever chosen to invoke the power.

DELORES DEL RIO

A mere twenty when she appeared on the screen in *Joanna* with Dorothy Mackail and Jack Mulhall, Delores Asunsolo was born in the Mexican state of Durango in 1906, the daughter of a wealthy banker. Discovered by director Edwin Carewe at a reception

As Charmaine in *What Price Glory?*, with Victor McLaglen and Edmund Lowe, 1927.

while visiting in Mexico City, Delores was the wife of Jaime del Rio, and although young in years she was wise enough not to be swept off her feet when the American offered her work in Hollywood. Her decision to do so had been carefully considered when she appeared in Los Angeles some months later to further investigate the offer before beginning the career that would soon cost her a husband and marriage—she and Jaime were divorced in 1928.

Even though she worked hard, Delores was a professional almost from the very beginning, and soon after making *Joanna* she was seen as the Russian peasant girl deserted by Rod LaRocque in *Resurrection.* The depth and intensity of her portrayal in a major role so early in a screen career silenced critics and proved that while Carewe might not be another Griffith, he had a keen eye for beauty and talent when he chose to exercise it. Miss del Rio next appeared as Charmaine, the French girl who shared her love with Edmund Lowe and Victor McLaglen in *What Price Glory,* a great box-office success. Its torrid love scenes are still remembered by those who saw this first screen adaptation of the popular Lawrence Stallings–Maxwell Anderson stage play.

Her role as the cigarette girl involved with a smuggling band in *Loves of Carmen* presented a heroine different in character from previous screen interpretations. Her passionate love for a famed toreador went unreturned, and in the end Delores paid for her sins and devotion with her life. It was a tailor-made role for the exotic delicacy of the Mexican actress just learning English and she never appeared more beautiful.

After the disappointing *Gateway to the Moon* with Walter Pigeon, her role in the tragic love story *Ramona* unquestionably stamped Delores as a gifted screen artist. While Warner Baxter's role in the film remained the central one, the emotional intensity with which Miss del Rio endowed her performance was a triumphant reaffirmation that *Resurrection* had not been merely a stroke of luck. Her portrayal of *Evangeline* was somewhat hampered by the story and Delores's career moved cautiously into talkies.

Flying Down to Rio in 1934 established her in the sound medium but someone decided that such beautiful perfection looked

***The Loves of Carmen*, with Don Alvarado, 1927.**

Warner Baxter and Delores in *Ramona,* 1928.

better modeling clothes than in solid dramatic roles and Miss del Rio spent the thirties in a series of trivia noted mainly for her many and varied costume changes. She married art director Cedric Gibbons in 1935 and just before making *Journey Into Fear* in 1943, they divorced. Delores then returned to her native Mexico where she quickly established herself as the country's leading screen actress, playing the roles Hollywood would not give her. In 1959, she married American producer Lewis Riley and reappeared in Hollywood films, looking as beautiful as ever.

Next to Fannie Ward, Delores del Rio has probably given more interviews over the years concerning her age and appearance than any other actress. It is unfortunate that what could have been an outstanding career in Hollywood never came to pass. Delores has seen fit to remain a Mexican star but has been making more and more forays into American television every year and it's always a delight to see this most professional (and beautiful) actress at work even on the small screen. Perhaps one day soon, Delores del Rio will finally become the object of numerous retrospective screenings at archives and film societies around the world. For my money, it's a tribute long overdue.

GERALDINE FARRAR

Thanks to Paramount's Adolph Zukor and Jesse Lasky, and Harry Aitken of Triangle, 1915 was a banner year for the move from stage to screen by theatrical talent. The cornerstone of Triangle's existence was to have been a great uplifting of the celluloid drama by famous stage actors and actresses; Zukor and Lasky had recovered from the ill effects of their earlier experiment with "Famous Players in Famous Plays" and now on a sounder financial footing, they tried a second time with more success. Among others, they signed Geraldine Farrar, considered one of the world's greatest prima donnas of the era and most certainly the finest American operatic talent of her time.

A Massachusetts girl of humble origin, Miss Farrar's talented voice was fortunately recognized by her parents and they were able to arrange a loan from a Boston philanthropist and patroness of the arts, Mrs. Annie Webb. The resulting money took the family abroad for two years while Geraldine studied under a succession of teachers, first in Paris and then in Berlin, making her debut there in 1901. The outstanding young singer returned home to embark upon a most successful and financially rewarding career, managing to repay the entire $30,000 loan in full by 1909. The next decade was filled with fresh operatic successes, including a recording contract which brought her rich vibrant voice to those unable to attend the Metropolitan Opera in person.

In the fall of 1914, Geraldine Farrar opened at the Met in *Carmen* and at the invitation of Morris Gest (David Belasco's son-in-law and her good friend), Jesse Lasky made an appearance.

Geraldine Farrar and husband Lou Tellegen.

Farrar and *Carmen* were all that Gest had indicated they would be and shortly, the producer had a new screen star and story under contract, with an option for additional films from her if all went well. Lasky figured that the combination of star and story would

Geraldine at the height of her career, 1919.

be sufficient to repay the gamble he was taking in bringing the singer to the screen, and while Geraldine was somewhat apprehensive about the value of a screen career, her mother and friends proved most persuasive. When the 1914–15 opera season ended,

With Wallace Reid in *Maria Rosa,* 1916.

the famed diva left for California ready to face the camera for the first time, only to find that William de Mille was still working on the screen treatment of *Carmen.* To pass the time until the script was ready, Lasky cast Farrar in a Spanish melodrama called *Maria Rosa* and she went to work for Cecil B. deMille, already a well-known director. Their relationship as director and star produced six good films for Famous Players over the next three years, earning money and prestige for both. Miss Farrar made her films in the off-season and managed to combine both careers with ease, with the screen work giving her an opportunity to rest her voice each year. But her contract with Lasky ended in 1917 and her problems had begun.

She had married a petulant and temperamental young actor in 1915 whose talent and box-office draw failed to agree with his own estimation of his worth. Unable to approach her success on-screen, Lou Tellegen was finally assigned to direct a picture and when it turned out badly, he quit; if Lou had not been Miss Farrar's husband, Lasky would probably have fired him months before. Tellegen convinced his wife not to renew her contract with

With the leering Tully Marshall in *Joan the Woman,* 1917.

Filled with striking symbolic scenes, *Joan the Woman* was de Mille's first great spectacle.

The Woman God Forgot **(1917), an Aztec story that closely rivaled *Joan the Woman* in spectacle.**

With Tom Santschi and Milton Sills in *Shadows,* 1918.

Geraldine and Milton Sills in *The Stronger Vow,* 1919.

Famous Players (where she was earning $4000 for 12 weeks work each year) and moved her to Sam Goldwyn's studio at Fort Lee, New Jersey. Geraldine made seven pictures for Goldwyn in 1918–19 and watched everything she had worked so hard to attain disappear during those two years. Tellegen virtually took over management of her career and became her leading man in the final three pictures she made for Goldwyn. Once he saw the billing, her husband's intense jealousy came to the surface and he caused Goldwyn no end of consternation over the matter. Unfortunately, Miss Farrar believed that a married couple should stand together and thus she sided with Tellegen. In addition, he collaborated with Willard Mack, a friend and neighbor who was Goldwyn's story editor, in determining the scripts which his wife would film. Miss Farrar's Goldwyn pictures were not up to the standards set by her previous work and the blame belongs equally with Tellegen's arrogant opinion of himself and Goldwyn's acquiescence to his wishes to keep peace in the studio. They failed to earn their keep at the box-office, and as a result Goldwyn was forced to ask Miss Farrar in 1919 to consider cancelling her contract, which still had two years remaining with a guarantee of $250,000 for 24 weeks of work. In a genuine and sincere gesture, she tore up the contract in front of the producer, refusing to take a cent in return. This stroke of good fortune on his part was one he never came to understand—people didn't do that for Sam Goldwyn very often.

While this resolution relieved Goldwyn, Miss Farrar soon learned that Tellegen had squandered her money almost as fast as she had earned it, a case remarkably similar to that of her good friend Pauline Frederick. In 1920, she agreed to make two features for Associated Exhibitors but *The Riddle: Woman* was her last screen appearance. Disappointed with the script and camera work, and constantly at odds with Edward Jose, the director, she broke her contract and left the screen for a brief return to the opera. Her mother died soon after and the star went into semi-retirement; she and Lou Tellegen had long since parted company. The career

***The World and Its Women,* with Lou Tellegen, 1919.**

Flame of the Desert, with Casson Ferguson, 1919.

A tender moment from one of the Diva's forgotten pictures.

which had started off so brightly in 1915 burned out after five short years and only 14 films.

But Geraldine Farrar's pictures had several positive effects. She had given the screen intensely dramatic portrayals in *Carmen* and *Joan the Woman* which subsequent actresses have found difficult to equal. Her name lent prestige to the motion picture and the "flickers" repaid her with thousands of dollars, making hers a household name and bringing her acting and singing to the attention of an entire nation who were not opera lovers. If Miss Farrar had one regret, it was that talking pictures had not been possible during her brief reign as a screen star. She had greatly enjoyed her acting and to have been able to combine it with her singing would have put the frosting on the cake.

PAULINE FREDERICK

One of the first of the famous stage names to enter movies in 1915, Pauline Frederick's career read like the script of an early soap opera. Although a recognized dramatic actress, Pauline herself once admitted that she was but an earthy, impractical woman who placed complete trust in each of her five husbands and lost every time. It's little wonder that she is best remembered today for her suffering portrayal in *Madame X,* a tragic melodrama that has served many actresses well, including Lana Turner, the latest of a lengthy line to rejuvenate a fading career with the hoary vehicle.

Born Pauline Beatrice Libby in Boston sometime between 1881 and 1885 (depending upon which source you accept), her professional stage debut came at New York's Knickerbocker Theatre on September 1, 1902 with a role in *The Rogers Brothers in Harvard.* She conquered Broadway, receiving her big break in *It Happened in Nordland* when Blanche Ring argued with Lew Fields and walked out of her starring role in his musical comedy. Pauline took over the role of Countess Pokota and the critics and fans responded with enthusiasm. Moving into serious acting, her career had carried Pauline to stardom when she met and married Frank Andrews, a New York architect, in 1909. She retired from the stage for three years to play the role of housewife. But domestic life didn't work out very well and in 1912, she was back again in front of the footlights, minus Andrews.

During the next three years Pauline built a solid reputation which led Adolph Zukor to sign her in 1914 for a screen version of Hall Caine's *The Eternal City.* Shot on location in Rome, the

PAULINE FREDERICK

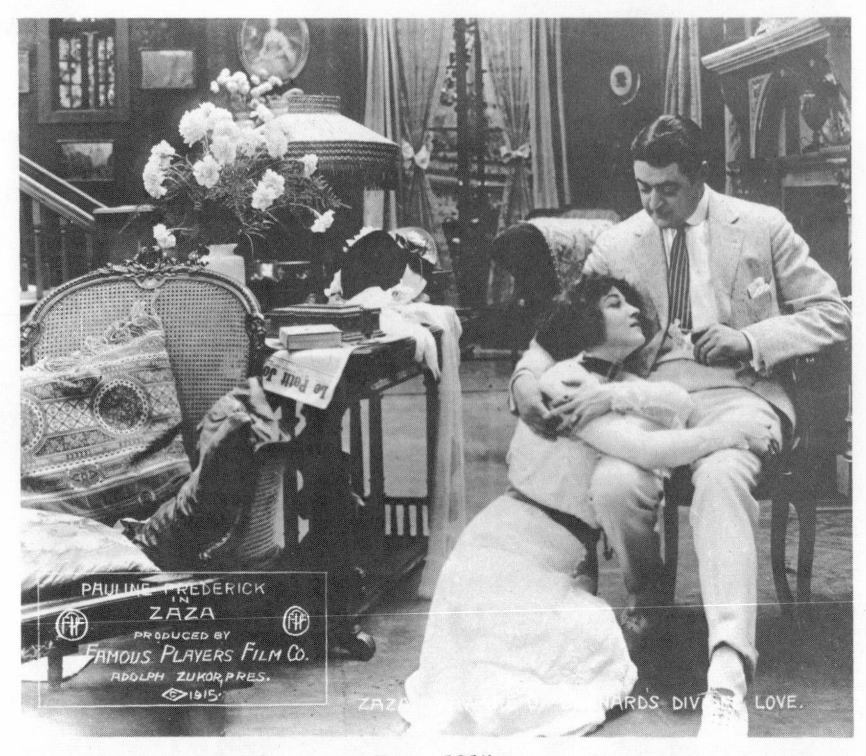

Zaza, 1915.

film was barely finished when war broke out in Europe and the crew was forced to leave. Released the following April, *The Eternal City* was a great success. Pauline's role was a sympathetic one, in contrast to the vixens she so often portrayed on the stage. Between 1915 and 1917, Pauline made 28 features for Famous Players, including *Sold, Zaza, Bella Donna* and *Resurrection.* Hugh Ford and Robert G. Vignola directed her pictures with a sure hand, portraying Pauline as the cold-hearted, calculating siren; the ultra-sophisticated adventuress whom fans took to their heart and for whom they emptied their pockets at the box-office. But Zukor sufficiently varied her roles so that the typing which was ruining Theda Bara at Fox did not follow Pauline. Films like *Audrey* and *The Love That Lives* cast her as a scrubwoman or simple country girl. An emotional actress, Pauline put everything she had into a first take and her directors soon learned to carefully plot out the scene in advance; rehearsals wasted her emotional fire and each retake she was required to do lessened the intensity of the scene.

Ashes of Embers, **1916.**

The Fear Woman, **1919.**

Madame **X (1920), Pauline's greatest melodramatic performance.**

With Clyde Fillmore in *Sting of the Lash.*

Her second marriage to Willard Mack in 1917 proved to be another mistake. Mack planned to open the Frederick Feature Film Company, with release through Goldwyn, but it failed to materialize and after further negotiations with Sam Goldwyn, he convinced Pauline to leave Famous Players when her contract was completed and join the Goldwyn forces, where he was scenario editor. It was here that Pauline was given *Madame X* as a story property, and under Frank Lloyd's direction she put across the sheer melodrama in a performance that many feel has not been matched since.

The marriage to Willard Mack broke up after 18 months, and Pauline moved to Goldwyn's Hollywood studio to complete her eight-picture contract. When these were finished, she moved to Robertson-Cole, where her manager had promoted both a healthy salary increase (to $7500 weekly) and script approval for Pauline. But few actors or actresses have the perspective to pick the correct stories for themselves, and in the course of filming her next six pictures Pauline practically disappeared from the screen. Fans who went to see the fiery dramatic talent in action were disappointed in these unconvincing pictures filmed from inadequate scripts and did not return for more.

With the completion of her R-C contract, Pauline returned to the legitimate stage and made her third marital error when she married C. A. Rutherford, a doctor and second cousin. Dr. Rutherford immediately gave up the practice of medicine to become her manager. This lasted but four months before they separated. As a manager, he spent her money and neglected her career and investments—as her husband, he generally made a nuisance of himself.

Through the rest of the decade, Pauline Frederick made only eight more films, each for a different company. *Married Flirts* and *Smouldering Fires* were proof positive to doubters that, given the right story and proper direction, Pauline was still a fine dramatic actress. The other woman may have won the man in the film, but Pauline walked away with the show. Clarence Brown directed *Smouldering Fires* and once reminisced that when she reported to work, Pauline was frightened and hesitant, but once her confidence returned after a few days on the set, she fell into the part with her old determination, giving a brilliant performance. This film earned Brown a contract with the Schenks to direct Norma Talmadge.

Pauline once more had her choice of scripts, and this time she exercised the power with extreme discretion. Making only an occasional film, she interspersed screen work with her stage tours and discovered that the public not only still remembered her, they still loved her. Mobbed abroad on personal appearance tours, she determined to once more revive her greatest success. In 1926, she formed a company to present *Madame X* and toured the country; the next year, she opened *Madame X* in London to packed houses and cheering curtain calls. Suffering from an asthmatical condition which restricted her activities considerably in the thirties, Pauline managed to fulfill her ambition to play Queen Elizabeth I on stage and made ten talkies, mostly as crochety or thoroughly despicable old women. She was about to sign contracts for a new play and a radio series when death came suddenly on September 19, 1938.

Donald Douglas put into words the feelings of her many fans with his editorial in the *Chicago Daily News,* which read in part:

> . . . when Pauline Frederick moved from the stage to the silent motion picture, her pantomime of gracious form and enamoring

Mae Busch and Pauline in *Married Flirts,* 1924.

On the set of *Married Flirts* with director Robert Vignola and cameraman Oliver Marsh.

gesture sufficed to invoke romance even without the bewitchment of her voice.

Only the other day she died, and thereby passed into that shadow world where the ghosts of dramatic art inhabit cloud castles and haunted groves more actual to the remembering mind than the harsh chaos which is too often reality. Therein she shall abide, not so much as herself, but as Elizabeth of England, Lady Rowena, Madame X, and the other parts she played—not, perhaps, with the divine fire, but with an enchantment answerable only to the sorcery of make-believe.

GRETA GARBO

Personally, I've never cared much for Greta Garbo's silent pictures, nor even for Miss Garbo herself. There, now that I've purged my soul in print, I'll be denounced as a heretic by every reader for profaning her name and image. But that wasn't really what I had in mind. There's no doubt that Greta Garbo was a fine actress, much finer indeed than the material with which she was given to work. Garbo's silent pictures were entertaining all right, but they were a disappointment she shared with her public. It was embarrassing that such a capable actress should be given soap opera melodramas as a showcase, especially when one considers that not only did the system allow this to happen, but condoned and even encouraged it, all in the name of stardom and the box-office!

Garbo herself was too lovely, too classical, too perfect to be real. It was almost as if a goddess had indeed descended from the heavens to walk among mortal men and perhaps the one thing which destroyed her illusion for many was this absolute perfection that the average male rarely encounters in real life—creating a lack of ability to identify with her. No matter what her dress or the angle from which she was seen, it was always the same cold glossy perfection. At least with Lillian Gish, there was an inner warmth that one encountered in real life, and with Norma Shearer, the external beauty did vary according to lighting and angle—again something one had experienced. But the variation with Garbo was minimal and thus unbelievable. Besides, all the girls I had known who fancied themselves femme fatales fell far, far short of the Garbo image. (Just for the record, let me say that Rita Hayworth affected me the same way in later years) . In spite of my own feelings for her

GRETA GARBO

silent pictures, Garbo's films were lavishly produced by M-G-M and made money here and abroad. And in those last days before the introduction of sound ruined many illusions, her pictures were superb examples of a particular style of opulent movie production that has accompanied the silent screen in a journey to undeserved obscurity.

Greta Garbo's discovery by Louis B. Mayer was quite acci-

With H. B. Warner in *The Torrent,* 1926.

***The Temptress,* 1926.**

Gilbert and Garbo in *Love,* 1927.

With Lowell Sherman in *The Divine Woman,* 1928.

Garbo and Conrad Nagel in *The Mysterious Lady,* 1928.

dental. On the first of his European trips during which Mayer usually combined business with pleasure (this time, *Ben Hur*'s production), he was persuaded to watch a screening of a recent film by director Maurice Stiller, *The Story of Gosta Berling*. His sharp eye for talent was captivated by the lovely young woman whose influence helped to redeem an alcoholic minister and when Mayer left

Berlin, he had made arrangements for both Stiller and Greta Gustafson to join M-G-M.

Greta was under contract at $400 weekly. She was first cast with Ricardo Cortez in *The Torrent,* an adaptation of an Ibanez novel. The story was standard—Spanish peasant girl becomes a great opera star and cannot marry the one man she loves. Monta Bell directed, which came as a shock to Stiller but he was given her next vehicle to do—for a short time. Another potboiler about a man ruined by his love for Garbo, *The Temptress* suffered from several problems. Fred Niblo replaced Stiller almost immediately, cast changes were instituted and footage shot by both men found its way into the final version. In spite of these problems, it met with critical acclaim before M-G-M substituted a completely ridiculous and out-of-character ending for the original melodramatic finish. But regardless of their defects, both films had allowed the magnetic and somewhat enigmatic Garbo personality to shine through and win audience approval.

Her romance with John Gilbert in *The Flesh and the Devil,* which followed, gave the film some torrid love scenes for its time. Publicity of the stars' undying devotion for each other brought patrons to theaters in seemingly unending lines, even though the story was about on the level of pulp magazine fiction in the best tradition established a few years before by Elinor Glyn. Some have voiced the suspicion that the entire affair began as a means of promoting the film; if so, it soon became a press agent's dream, as Garbo was refusing to work until the studio revised her contract to $5000 weekly.

Settling their contract problems, M-G-M rushed Garbo into *Love* (a rewrite of *Anna Karenina* by Tolstoy), taking determined advantage of the red-hot romance by again casting Gilbert as her lead. Their ardor cooled considerably after this film and the two went their separate ways, with Greta appearing in *The Divine Woman.* Stiller had stood on the sidelines long enough, watching and waiting to no avail. Not allowed to direct his former star, the director returned to Europe a disillusioned and sick man. After his departure, Garbo's personality became more and more withdrawn and she stopped resisting Mayer's scripts. *The Mysterious Lady, A Woman of Affairs* and *Wild Orchids* followed, then a trip home to Sweden. Stiller had died during the filming of *Wild Orchids* and Garbo left Hollywood in December 1928. She made two more silent pictures after her return in 1929, *The Single Standard* and *The Kiss,* before the studio decided to try her in a talkie.

Garbo and Gilbert in *A Woman of Affairs,* 1929.

***A Woman of Affairs,* 1929.**

***Wild Orchids,* 1929, with Lewis Stone and Nils Asther.**

The effect of sound on Garbo's career had been a topic of heavy speculation for over a year. Her husky Swedish accent might destroy the illusion of femininity M-G-M had worked so hard to create, or so the studio reasoned, and the fact that sooner or later she must face the challenge was one approached with great trepidation. Her talking pictures debut was carefully considered and Eugene O'Neill's play *Anna Christie* was finally settled upon as being ideal; as its heroine was the slightly worn daughter of a Swedish sea captain, this provided the excuse for her accent, as well as giving Garbo a strong dramatic role with which to work. All the elements were there under Clarence Brown's direction. The M-G-M publicity department began its GARBO SPEAKS! campaign and the picture was completely successful. Thus Garbo moved into the sound era full of confidence.

After this auspicious beginning in talkies, Greta made 13 more pictures, ending with *Two-Faced Woman* in 1941. Many of her scripts were much more worthy of her talents than the silent films had been. Her accent was never completely lost, but it did become subdued and added an air of mystery and intrigue to the already legendary screen goddess.

There were many good bits and pieces in even the worst of her silent films, and it is unarguable that Garbo stands among the very top of her profession on the basis of comparatively few pictures (27 in 16 years). Never one to seek publicity (her battles over her privacy while at M-G-M are also legendary), Garbo stepped out of movies and has shunned the limelight ever since. Occasionally, a new picture of her pops up in the newspaper or a magazine after some photographer has followed her for days, and her career comes flooding back for those who remember.

But the legend of Greta Garbo lives primarily in the minds of the faithful, and from time to time it is perpetuated by revival showings of some of her pictures, usually the talkies. Garbo not only speaks, she is immortal—thanks to the tiny images on a slender strip of celluloid.

LILLIAN GISH

Few will argue the contention that Lillian Gish stands virtually alone as the greatest of the silent screen's heroines. A consummate actress, her cinematic performances were often artistic triumphs as well as fascinating screen entertainment; audiences seldom left a Gish picture without some new insight into the many facets of her talent. Possessing a native intuition which she brought to bear on each new role, Lillian Gish was able to succeed where other screen actresses failed. This quality, much desired by every serious actress, was a rarity given to only a few and its proper application remained an even greater rarity. Often compared by her contemporaries with Duse and Bernhardt, Miss Gish remains today as the Helen Hayes of the American screen, occupying a position in her art often sought but never attained by others.

And yet it was not a great insight or artistic yearning which brought her to the screen; she and her sister Dorothy arrived at the old New York Biograph studio on East 14th Street in 1912 from simple economic necessity, as had so many others before them. The movies offered a certain security lacking in theatrical engagements —there were no slack seasons for those working in the youthful "flickers." The fragile Gish features were heightened and emphasized on the large screen and Lillian's delicate beauty soon became that of the archtypical Griffith heroine and her account of mastering the art of screen acting, as described in her recent autobiography (with Ann Pinchot), *The Movies, Mr. Griffith and Me,* makes delightful reading.

Her early work for Griffith was briefly overshadowed by the presence of Mary Pickford, a friend from stage days who had invited

LILLIAN GISH

the sisters to visit her at Biograph and whose immense popularity with audiences would rival Lillian's artistic achievements in years to come, yet the commercial appeal of Pickford in no way detracted from Miss Gish's accomplishments. Her films soon made their share of money, and with Mary's final departure from Griffith and Biograph, Lillian Gish came into her own in films like *The Unseen Enemy, The Musketeers of Pig Alley, Battle of the Sexes* and *Home Sweet Home.*

***The Musketeers of Pig Alley,* 1912.**

Attracted to Griffith's abundant talent by training and temperament, Lillian remained with him through his years with Mutual and Triangle. While few of her roles during this period emphasized or even required much acting ability, she managed to turn in sensitive performances in spite of the slight material handed her. Her outstanding performance as Elsie Stoneman in *The Birth of a Nation* was Lillian's last challenging role until Griffith left Triangle, and those years with Triangle left no particular impression on her career. Her Triangle Plays received reasonably good trade reviews at the time, but because of Triangle's insistence that only contract theaters could play its films, her pictures were not widely distributed. But during these years, Lillian was undergoing a process of maturation in her acting and emerged a near-complete artist beginning with *Hearts of the World* in 1917. She gave superb accounts of herself as the rural sweetheart in *True Heart Susie* and the battered waif of *Broken Blossoms,* two very different roles. By the time she made *Way Down East* in 1920, Lillian Gish had no peers on the screen. It was her performance alone that kept the hackneyed old melodrama believable.

Miss Gish's association with Griffith lasted until the completion of *Orphans of the Storm* in 1922; beyond that point, D. W. Griffith could contribute nothing further to her career. Her mastery of screen acting had surpassed his needs, but the parting was an amicable one and she has always keenly treasured their many years of collaboration. After leaving Griffith her screen appearances during the twenties were much less frequent and more carefully chosen, allowing Lillian the opportunity to portray mature heroines in contrast to the saccharine sweetness and innocence of her Griffith years. Yet today, her reputation still rests heavily on the Griffith years—an interesting commentary on her career, for with Griffith, the story was the key. Few if any of his pictures could be considered as starring vehicles in the usual sense for one or two members of the cast, yet if Lillian Gish was featured in the picture, it is usually recalled as one of hers.

After completing *The White Sister* and *Romola* on location in

As Elsie Stoneman in *The Birth of a Nation,* 1915. Henry B. Walthall as "The Little Colonel."

***True Heart Susie,* 1917.**

Italy for Charles Duell, Lillian returned to the United States where in 1925 she signed a six-picture, $800,000 contract with M-G-M. Her first was a film version of Puccini's opera *La Boheme;* an exceedingly fine picture in spite of the fact that it left costar John Gilbert slightly unnerved. The dashing romantic lead could not quite grasp Lillian's conception of her role and was thus totally dismayed over her refusal to kiss him on-screen. So was Louis B.

***The White Sister,* 1924.**

As Letty in *The Wind,* Lillian's last M-G-M picture.

Lillian confers with director Fred Niblo and cameraman Oliver Marsh.

Mayer, who couldn't see wasting Gilbert's great talent (in view of the success of his previous picture, *The Big Parade*) and ordered a different ending shot. *The Scarlet Letter* came next, despite Mayer's objection to the advent of the adulteress Hester Prynne as an M-G-M heroine; it proved to be one of the finest pictures of 1926. These were followed by *Annie Laurie* and *The Enemy,* two good films but somewhat less popular than her first pair.

The M-G-M contract came to an end by mutual agreement after Lillian's performance for Victor Seastrom (who also directed *The Scarlet Letter*) in *The Wind,* a most unusual and masterful but nevertheless depressing tale of life in the American Southwest. While Miss Gish had added a large degree of luster to the M-G-M heaven of stars, she had also become too "artistic" for its taste. Crew and cast admired and respected Miss Gish for her knowledge of their crafts and the unusually keen vigor with which she approached her work; even directors King Vidor and Seastrom were impressed with her integrity and creative interest, treating her with deference and accepting her suggestions. But in the case of *The Wind,* even

From *Annie Laurie*, 1927.

the sales department was unsure of quite what to do with it or how it could best be marketed and as film sales were the foundation of a studio's success, the sales people often won the day. While the film sat on the shelf awaiting some decision, sound made its appearance and finally sound effects were dubbed, a happy ending substituted for the original grim one and *The Wind* was released; Miss Gish had long since departed.

While Lillian worked occasionally in talkies, she regarded the addition of sound as the destruction of a universal language. Her devotion to the silent film led her back to the theatre, where she continued to amaze audiences with her powerful but sensitive portrayals. Now and then, she is seen on television today and watching her at work, even in the small roles, is a genuine delight and pleasure for those of us who remember good acting, and an education for those brought up on the "method" and other eccentric schools of acting. As the silent film has slipped into the past forever, so eventually will Lillian Gish, yet it is safe to say that the greatness of both the actress and her medium will not be surpassed for a long time to come.

ELAINE HAMMERSTEIN

Like junkyard magnate Louis B. Mayer, Pittsburgh diamond broker Lewis J. Selznick was one of the "Johnny-Come-Lately" producers who attempted to carve out a production and distribution empire comparable to those already created by Adolph Zukor, William Fox and Carl Laemmle. But unlike Mayer, who would eventually head M-G-M, his success in doing so was limited, even though he gave his competition a bad case of nerves for a few years. Selznick had come into the industry via Universal but rose to prominence at World Film, where he acquired the services of the stunning Clara Kimball Young. He shortly parted company with World, but took Miss Young with him, beginning the acquisition of stars that would eventually allow him to challenge the power of the entrenched moguls with his Select Pictures.

Zukor bought out Select in hopes that Selznick would take his leave of the industry, but with a substantial profit in his pocket and nothing to do, Selznick's next venture was the creation of Selznick Pictures. In order to compete with a regular release schedule, he produced some pictures and bought other titles sufficient to meet his needs. And so for a few years immediately following World War I, Selznick was a contender along with Goldwyn and Mayer, but never one who breathed dangerously close to the leaders.

Among the several stars who carried the banner of Selznick Pictures to the screen was the young and attractive daughter of Arthur Hammerstein, the well-known theatrical producer. Born in Philadelphia in 1897, Elaine Hammerstein's close connection with the theatre almost guaranteed her success in show business, with

ELAINE HAMMERSTEIN

***The Country Cousin,* 1919.**

or without talent. In spite of making a most favorable impression in *High Jinks,* her first musical comedy role, Elaine disliked the stage and turned to the screen for a career. She appeared in several of the Robert Warwick and Ralph Ince features which World released during 1915–17. Shortly after he left World, Elaine found L. J. Selznick with contract in hand, eager to sign her—Hammerstein was a name which could be easily exploited.

The Selznick Pictures were lavish and often flashy expositions of the screen's art and Elaine proved to be a refreshing personality in films like *Country Cousin, The Daughter Pays* and *The Miracle of Manhatten.* Each actress seems to have one particular role she enjoys playing, and with Elaine it was the society drama that gave her an opportunity to portray both the lady of quality and the fallen woman. A fashionable dresser who loved clothes, Elaine entertained with as many changes of chic costume as possible in her pictures. While she made some thirty films before retiring from the screen in 1926 to marry insurance executive James W. Kays, Elaine was not particularly in love with her acting and took her career rather lightly, refusing to join the usual Hollywood social whirl.

What made Elaine Hammerstein's films so enjoyable? This same lightheartedness with which she regarded her career came across boldly on screen. Here was an actress who bore her distinguished name without pretensions, and even in the deepest of melodramatic moments seemed to be saying, "It's only a great big make-believe world." With few exceptions, life as portrayed on the silver screen during the early twenties was a far cry from reality and Elaine's refusal to treat it otherwise worked heavily in her favor.

She did take special pride in her role as Queen Flavia in *Rupert of Hentzau.* In addition to enjoying the lavish costuming of this Ruritanian romance, she turned in the most memorable performance of her career. With veterans Bert Lytell and Bryant Washburn among the "all-star" cast, which also included Irving Cummings, Claire Windsor and Lew Cody, Elaine had costars who were thoroughly professional (circumstances she had not always

***The Daughter Pays,* 1920.**

The Shadow of Rosalie Byrnes, 1920.

With Hallam Cooley in *One Week of Love,* 1922.

***Reckless Youth*, 1922.**

been as fortunate to enjoy). Under the direction of Victor Heerman, who still recalls vivid memories of this particular screen adventure, Elaine worked long hours to develop the characterization that Heerman demanded. It proved to be a worthwhile effort, for *Rupert of Hentzau* was one of the more memorable of the Selznick Pictures, even though its plot line was a rather hoary variation on *The Prisoner of Zenda* theme.

Elaine's retirement from the screen was genuine and she never regretted it. She led an active life involving considerable travel. In fact, it was on one of her Mexican trips that an automobile accident claimed Elaine Hammerstein's life in August 1948. Her films are rarely seen these days, and while Elaine was never a star of the first magnitude, she did lend a sparkle to the early twenties.

JUANITA HANSEN

After appearing for six highly successful years as the greatest of the serial queens, Pearl White left Pathé in 1919 to star in features for William Fox. With Pearl went Pathé's Mother Lode, for she had made a fantastic amount of money for the firm, and her replacement became a matter of grave concern. When Pearl had balked at her salary in 1917, Mollie King was quickly groomed as her successor. However Miss King had wisely decided against the life of a serial heroine, married and returned to occasional feature work. Pathé now doubted that Pearl could be replaced at any price.

Enter Juanita Hansen. A rather shapely blonde by 1919 standards, Miss Hansen had joined the entertainment world immediately after high school, appearing as a chorus girl and then in bit roles for Famous Players-Lasky (*The Love Riot*) before contracting with the American Film Manufacturing Company. An intensely ambitious young lady, Juanita wanted stardom at any price and worked hard to earn the leading role in American's 1916 preparedness serial, *The Secret of the Submarine.* But American was not a star-making organization, so her good work in this chapter play went unnoticed. Juanita continued her quest in 1917 with Mack Sennett's Keystone Comedies, where she spent much of her time smiling attractively for the camera instead of acting. Sennett's lot was filled with pretty girls and Juanita was unable to break out of the mold, so she moved to Universal where she carried the lead in *The Brass Bullet* the following year. No great fanfare resulted from this part and Juanita resigned herself to the role of Princess Elyata in the Warner Brothers' jungle epic, *The Lost City.*

Released in early 1920 both as a serial (*The Lost City*) and as

JUANITA HANSEN

a seven-reel feature (*The Jungle Princess*), her wild animal adventures proved to be very successful for the Warners. The film showed an actress who had not completely muted the over-emotional responses characteristic of the 1912–14 school of screen acting—a fact that failed to bother serial fans, who flocked to the theaters to see what perils she would encounter in the 15 episodes. But by the time she had started filming "The Lost City," Juanita had concluded

***The Secret of the Submarine,* 1916.**

that talent could carry her no further; her career lacked the necessary "muscle."

Hearing rumors of Miss White's eminent departure from Pathé, Juanita met with Louis Gasnier, an old acquaintance and one who had sufficient contact within Pathé (Gasnier had produced *The Perils of Pauline* and several other profitable serials for Pathé release) to help her. The combination of Gasnier's influence and Miss Hansen's persuasiveness convinced Pathé, and in early 1920 Juanita began filming *The Phantom Foe* with Warner Oland. She was to make only one other cliff hanger, *The Yellow Arm.* Both were directed by Bertram Millhauser, a talented writer with a flair for the melodramatic who turned director for her debut as a Pathé star. Pathé provided Juanita with good story material for her serials (Frank Leon Smith wrote one; Millhauser the other) and its usual fine production values, but soon found its new star unable to work with any degree of regularity; the blonde successor to "The Lady Daredevil of The Fillums" was discovered to be a narcotics addict.

With Billy Armstrong in *A Royal Rogue,* one of Juanita's 1917 Keystone Comedies.

Juanita often told the story of how she was introduced to drugs at a Hollywood party as a joke, but she never quite made the date clear, so it is impossible to tell how long she had been addicted

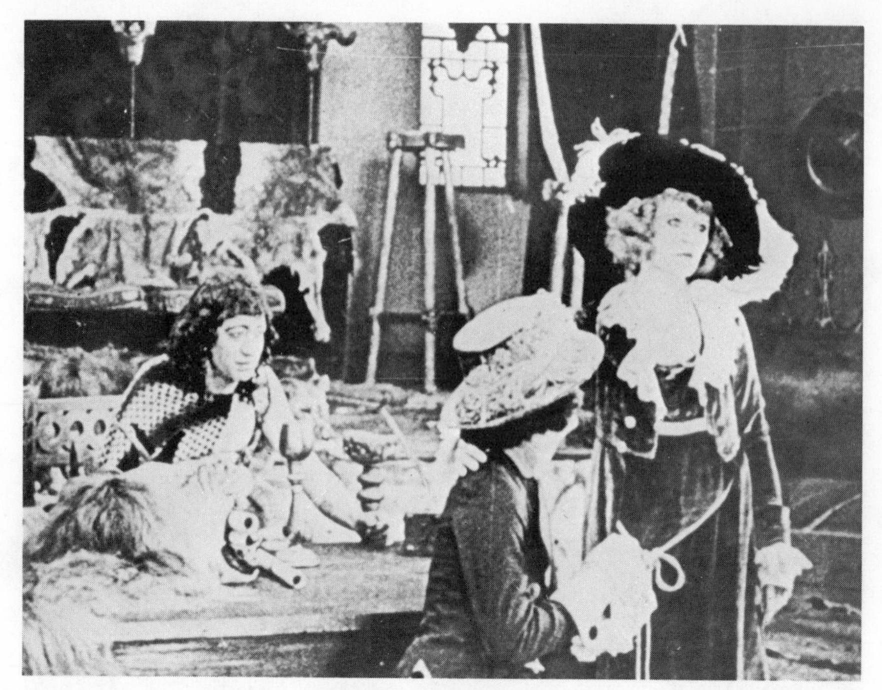

The Lost City, 1920.

Taken prisoner countless times in *The Lost City,* Juanita grew accustomed to meeting danger with a wild-eyed stare.

prior to joining Pathé. We do know that she spent $2500 in 1920 to effect "the cure," which lasted all of three days. Although her salary at Pathé reached $1250 weekly, she needed all of it to support the habit and her periodic attempts at shaking it. But by the time she had finished *The Yellow Arm,* narcotics had woven its spell around her tightly and Juanita was a nervous wreck, unable to work even had Pathé wanted her to. In the wake of the scandals which broke in Screenland during 1920–21, Pathé could not afford to keep their new serial queen on the payroll; had it become public knowledge that she was an addict the company's reputation for providing good clean entertainment would have been irretrievably tarnished and she could have proven to be a financial liability too great to retain under contract.

After undergoing several "cures," Juanita announced her return to the serial screen in 1923, but it never came to pass. She was too undependable for any producer to hire, no one would finance her own company in light of her reputation and her personal

Wallace McCutcheon, Tom Goodwin, Juanita, and William N. Bailey look aghast as Joe Cuny puts the finger on Warner Oland in *The Phantom Foe,* 1920, her first Pathé serial.

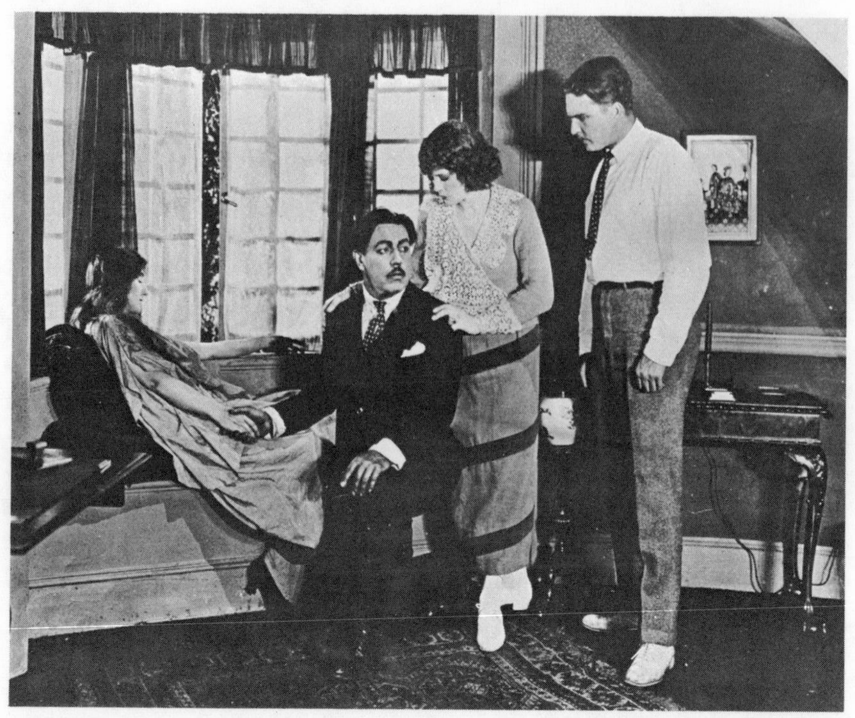

Nina Cassavent, Warner Oland, Juanita, and William N. Bailey in *The Phantom Foe*, 1920.

financial status was bleak. She continued to make the rounds of sanitariums and vaudeville houses until a "cure" at Lexington, Kentucky, finally took and Juanita returned to New York in 1928 for a part in Lou Sobol's *The High Hatters.* But then tragedy struck again. Nearly scalded to death by an accident in the shower room of her hotel, the actress was given morphine to relieve the immense pain of third degree burns over one half of her body, and in the slow process of recovery she was addicted once more.

Bringing suit against the hotel for negligence, she was awarded $118,000, $93,000 of which went for medical expenses and the remainder for drugs to support the habit. Years later, Juanita was to reduce the amount paid the hospital whenever she discussed the subject, adding it onto the amount paid for drugs and increasing the horror of her addiction for the interviewer. Six more years of wandering and various "cures" followed, until a 1934 stay in an Oakland, California sanitarium worked. With her screen and stage

Warner Oland, William N. Bailey, and Juanita in her second Pathé serial and final screen appearance, *The Yellow Arm,* 1921.

career in ruins, her beauty faded and her figure gone, there was not much left for Juanita Hansen. By now a known addict and watched by police wherever she went, Miss Hansen took to the cheaper carnival circuits and toured the country peddling her emotional anti-drug message to anyone who would pay 15 cents to listen. Dressed in black, with a huge cross and sprig of flowers adorning her neckline, Juanita cut a pathetic figure, this former golden girl of the screen who held interviews in a hollow voice and spoke empty words which centered solely upon her affliction and the sordid side of her Hollywood days. Her last years were spent in obscurity as a clerk for the Southern Pacific Railroad and in 1961, she was found dead in her Hollywood apartment.

Juanita Hansen's story was one of the more tragic of the silent screen heroines, for she had possessed the beauty, brains and sufficient talent to reign as a leading serial queen well into the twenties. One might even suppose that she could have tempered her acting technique to adapt to the changing audience tastes in the latter twenties, when cliff hanger heroines merely presented an attractive object of interest for the serial heroes. The youthful Miss Hansen showed a promise far beyond that which she ever managed to fulfill; watching the pleasing personality which she projected in her early work dance across the screen once more today, it is not even difficult to imagine that she might have crossed paths with a producer who could have polished her image, presenting her to the public in dramatic feature roles which would have considerably widened her horizons and greatly enhanced her career.

For a brief time, Juanita Hansen had everything working in her favor, until the intense and uncontrollable craving for drugs blotted out the ambition which had carried her from chorus line to marquee billing. While Juanita was really a victim of herself who paid an ungodly price for a moment of success, in a larger sense, she was the victim of a society which denounced drugs, condemned addiction and hounded the user, but refused to acknowledge its responsibility in making rehabilitation a reality.

LEATRICE JOY

One of Cecile B. deMille's favorite actresses, Leatrice Joy had a long and varied career on the screen, but she's best remembered for her work with deMille—as a mannish businesswoman who had no time for love or emotional display, or the spoiled society mannequin who faced life with a studied indifference. Usually a confrontation with near-disaster involving the stark reality of human nature broke her icy reserve to reveal a human being underneath. Leatrice cut a most impressive figure on-screen during these years, usually appearing either in smartly tailored male attire with bobbed hair or elegantly garbed in the latest luxurious creations of Adrian. Her roles in *The Ten Commandments, Manslaughter* and *Vanity* gave Miss Joy an opportunity to indulge in some pretty heavy melodrama, but there was another and lighter side to this versatile actress's nature.

It had all started in New Orleans, where she was born in 1897. Her formal education was remarkably similar to that of many other silent screen actresses—she was placed in a convent school in New Orleans. Once her education was completed in 1915, Leatrice left the cloistered atmosphere of Sacred Heart Academy to join the Virginia Brissac Stock Company where she undertook ingenue roles. About the same time, local businessmen formed the Nola Film Company, hoping to make New Orleans a center of the growing film industry. Reading Nola's advertisement for a leading lady, Leatrice applied for the position, and when she was chosen over scores of applicants it came as no great surprise to her; with the confidence of youth, the die was cast. Movies were much more fascinating, more profitable and held a greater career potential to

LEATRICE JOY

***Bunty Pulls the Strings,* 1920**

the young would-be actress than the stage could offer, and although Nola soon closed its doors Leatrice had decided upon her career. As luck would have it (in the best tradition of Hollywood success stories), the family moved to Wilkes-Barre, Pennsylvania, where Leatrice arrived in time to work in the Black Diamond Comedies being filmed there for Paramount release. It was a stroke of fortunate timing, as the Black Diamond studio also shuttered its doors within a few months, and once again our heroine was out of work. But now she had "experience" and could claim a certain distinction as the leading lady of two film companies, even though both had since gone out of business. The time was now ripe for a move to Hollywood and permanent work.

Leatrice arrived on the West Coast at the same time Billy West and his King Bee troupe of funmakers moved their activities from New York to California. King Bee was always in need of attractive but inexpensive talent and she was hired to support Billy in *Slaves,* a comedy with no subtitles. Working with the Chaplin imitator in several of his other comedies over the next year, Leatrice provided

Leatrice didn't go in for the long, lingering kiss.

the center of contention over whom Billy and Oliver Hardy fought, entering into the spirit of the slapstick melee with a talented enthusiasm. To this day, Billy maintains that Leatrice Joy was the finest leading lady he ever worked with, and dramatic talent notwithstanding she could have become a clever comedienne, had that been her ambition.

But Miss Joy had plans, and while comedy had helped her along the road, she could not see it as a way of life. After working with West, Leatrice made the rounds of the studio casting offices and eventually landed a part in *Bunty Pulls the Strings.* Her appearance in this role broke the ice, and by 1921 Leatrice Joy had more than enough work to keep her busy. Signed to a Paramount contract, she was also a popular loan-out player, and throughout the twenties

Two scenes from *Saturday Night* (1922), with Jack Mower.

Leatrice was one of Cecil B. de Mille's favorite actresses in the twenties.

she graced the screen for Goldwyn and others in a great variety of roles, ranging from light comedy to heavy melodrama.

The biggest boost to her career came in 1922 when deMille

Silent Partner **(1923), with Owen Moore.**

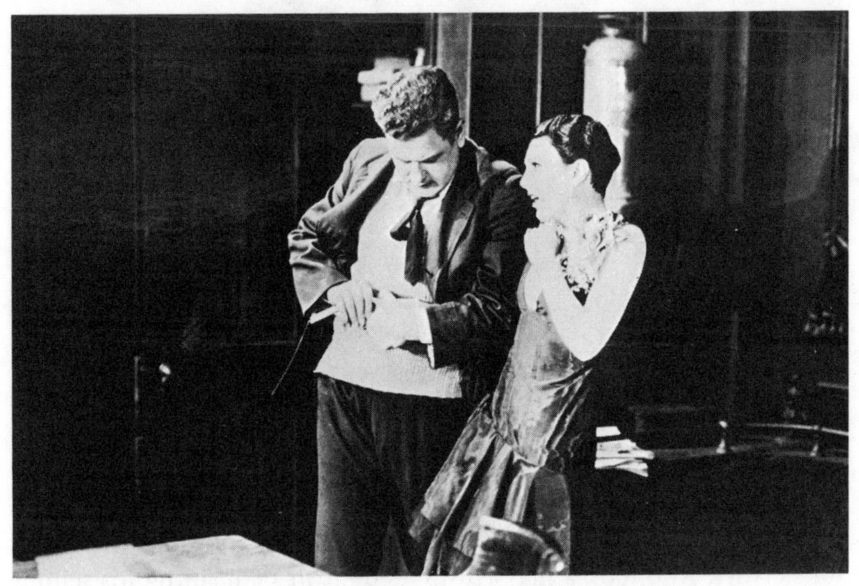

Manhandled by Alan Hale in *Vanity,* 1927.

The Water Lily.

cast Leatrice as the star of *Manslaughter,* an overly dramatic affair that made money at the box-office and further alienated the director's critics, who took a masochistic delight in bemoaning his sellout of the artistry, which they were all certain he commanded, to com-

With Nils Asther in *The Blue Danube,* 1928.

mercialism. But deMille was a showman first and foremost; he realized that commercialism sold more theater tickets than artistry, and during the rest of the twenties he and Leatrice Joy combined to sell their share and then some.

Leatrice's personal life was also stormy and melodramatic during this period; she had married a young unknown named Jack Gilbert in 1919. Gilbert's star had just started to ascend under the sure hand of Thomas H. Ince and his divorce from his former wife wasn't quite completed when he married Leatrice in Tijuana. Their return to Hollywood occasioned so much gossip that the couple were forced to separate and await the proper legal termination of his marriage. Some months later, they were properly remarried. Gilbert was a good actor, but he wasn't to hit his stride until the mid-twenties, by which time he and Leatrice had parted company amicably; Jack's ego couldn't live with a woman who was more successful than he.

Leatrice made some talking pictures, but it was the silent cinema which remained her first love and while she occasionally talks about the old days at various social gatherings in the Greenwich, Connecticut, area where she's now retired, she is very content with her present role as a former film star who helped create the golden age of the movies.

Leatrice Joy
John Gilbert
m Tijuana
write
send story on Bessie

ALICE JOYCE

Alice Joyce has always been a great favorite, not only for her considerable talent but also because of her striking appearance. Projecting a Mona Lisa quality of mystery, this serenely beautiful woman was one of the outstanding entertainers of the silent screen. With her finely drawn, exquisite features, she reminded one of a lovely, fragile Dresden doll. If any actress ever had a valid claim to the title of *Madonna of the Silent Screen,* it was Miss Joyce.

A product of Kansas City, Missouri, Alice left school to support her mother; she began work as a telephone operator when she was only 13. With a quiet charm that gave the young girl a look of maturity far beyond her years, she was a natural for modeling and it was inevitable that someone would discover her. When Alice joined Kalem in 1910, she left a highly successful career posing for photographers and artists to work in the movies.

Kalem was deeply involved at the time with Civil War and western dramas and Miss Joyce's career began in supporting roles at a time when player casts were not identified for the audiences. But fans quickly became attached to her sad and lonesome smile, and as Kalem grew in importance, so did Alice's reputation; known to fans as *The Kalem Girl,* Miss Joyce adorned the screen nearly every week, becoming the pioneer producer's most valuable feminine star. In 1913, *Motion Picture Story Magazine* conducted its second annual poll of top screen favorites and Alice was the only female to place in the first five positions. Her early association with Gene Gauntier, Sidney Olcott, George Melford, Carlyle Backwell and others of the Kalem stock company proved invaluable in giving her the rudiments of screen acting, for while a wealth of talent existed under

Alice Joyce and Tom Moore in *The Artist's Sacrifice*, an early Kalem.

its banner in the early years, no other actress on any of the several Kalem lots had such an extensive and successful career as Alice Joyce.

In five years with Kalem, Miss Joyce was seen mostly in romantic and dramatic leads. There was a certain dignity and character about her which made Alice unsuitable for the comic parts in which Ruth Roland and Marin Sais were seen. Nor was she a rugged outdoors type like Helen Holmes and Helen Gibson; Alice was at her best in a drawing room situation, graciously garbed in high fashion clothes. When Kalem featured their star on the popular postcards sold to fans at the time, they dressed her in a $3000 gown and decorated it with jewelry supposedly worth $1 million. This particular portrait sold millions of cards.

When Vitagraph bought out Kalem, Alice became one of its top box-office attractions. Kalem had brought Miss Joyce popularity; she was instantly recognized by moviegoers, and during its last days Kalem reissued many of her earlier subjects along with a less-

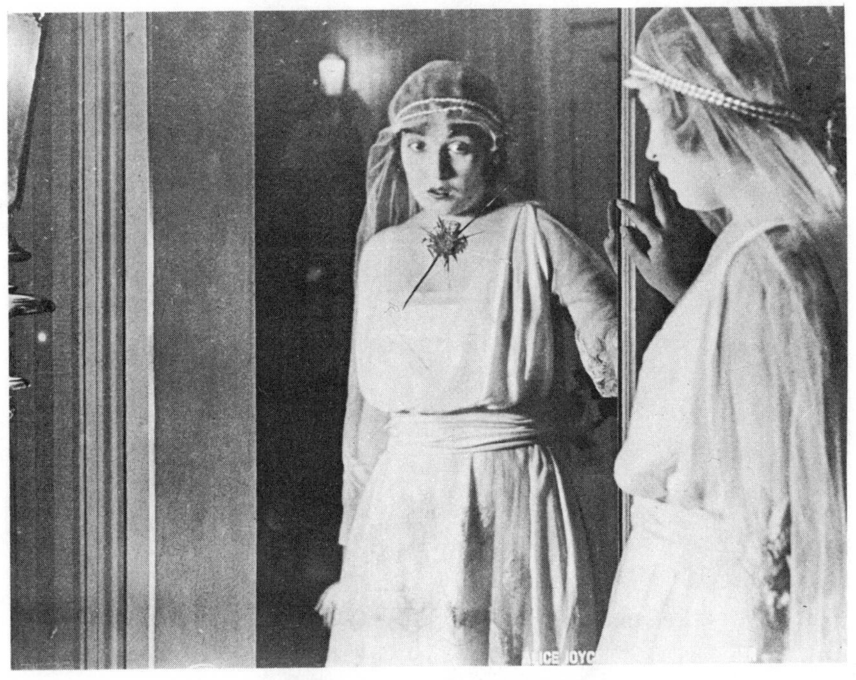

***The Inner Chamber*, 1916.**

***The Lion and the Mouse*, 1919.**

Alice and Belle Bennett in *Stella Dallas,* 1926.

With Ronald Colman in *Stella Dallas,* 1926.

frequent schedule of new releases. But it was Vitagraph which brought her real fame, casting Alice in features like *The Lion and the Mouse* and *The Third Degree*. Her salary reached $3000 weekly, and while the popular actress had numerous opportunities to jump her contract and sign with other producers eager to pay her a much larger salary, Alice Joyce had the good sense to realize that few stars who had done so found it really profitable in the long run.

A marriage to actor Tom Moore had ended in divorce, and in 1920 Alice wed James B. Regan Jr., a wealthy hotelman. She left the screen in the early twenties to play the role of devoted wife, but domestic bliss did not work out and although she and Regan did not part company until 1932, Alice soon returned in front of the cameras to resume her career.

Miss Joyce had some very good roles in the twenties which called upon the vitality and inner strength she was so capable of projecting, and while not a superstar like Pickford or Gish, Alice did turn in fine performances in films like *The Green Goddess*

Alice and Clara Bow, *Dancing Mothers,* 1926.

The Noose, 1928

(playing opposite George Arliss in both the 1923 silent and 1929 talkie versions), *Our Dancing Mothers* and *The Noose.* Although still a youthful actress, she was quite often cast as a wife or mother, roles that took full advantage of her mature appearance. As Clara

With Ralph Forbes in *Beau Geste,* 1927.

Bow's mother in *Our Dancing Mothers,* she was the wife who felt that she had been taken for granted too often by her family and left home to fall in love with another man. In an unusual ending for that day, Alice had not returned home at the final fadeout. *The Noose* found her as the wife of a district attorney who built a murder case against a young man, without realizing that the suspect was her son by a former marriage. As the script called for the mother not to reveal her secret, Alice made the most of some rather good dramatic moments in this variation on the *Madame* X theme.

Alice worked on and off in talkies until 1933, when she married director Clarence Brown and settled down to raise her two daughters, one by her marriage to Tom Moore and the other by Regan. The union with Brown ended with a 1945 divorce and Alice spent her last years associated with various women's groups in charitable work. Death came in 1955 after a lingering illness caused by a blood disease. To her fans, it almost seemed that Alice Joyce was too beautiful to age and would certainly escape The Grim Reaper. But while she proved to be mortal after all, a thin strip of celluloid became her immortality, and for those who care, her timeless beauty can be seen and appreciated today as it was when the movies and she were young.

BARBARA LA MARR

If ever a woman was cursed by her beauty, it was Raetha Watson, remembered by screen fans as Barbara La Marr. Listening to her friends and acquaintances tell the story, La Marr's life was a nightmare concocted by a sadistic imp from the nether world. To be sure, it was a short life, but Barbara packed ages of torment into less than three decades and five quick years on the screen. Her first public appearance was made in front of a Los Angeles judge, who sent the runaway teenager back to her San Fernando home with the admonishment that she was "too beautiful" to be alone in the world. That the judge had excellent taste is not in doubt; his opinion appears to have been shared by many others. Upon her return home, Reatha promptly eloped with a wealthy young rancher, only to leave him and file for an annulment almost as soon as they were married.

A year or so later, she married again, this time to a brilliant Los Angeles attorney. The newlyweds were very happy but some women manage to attract trouble; her new husband already had a wife and three children, who shortly had him arrested for bigamy. Pleading that this nubile child's beauty had driven him completely out of his mind, the court ordered him to undergo a medical examination, which attributed his real problem not to Barbara's beauty, but to a blood clot on the brain. The doctors operated and he died.

Bewildered and heartbroken at this turn of events, Barbara next appeared in public as a dancer at the San Francisco World's Fair in 1915. Her partner, a wealthy young scion from the social register, succumbed to her charms and, unable to resist his persistent

***The Eternal City*, 1924.**

and ardent pursuit, Barbara gave in and they were married. Within months after the ceremony, he was sent to San Quentin for check forgery, an act which he passed off as the only way he could afford to keep Barbara in the manner he felt she deserved; his parents had cut off his funds when they married.

La Marr went back to dancing, arriving on the screen as Douglas Fairbanks's personal choice for the role of Milady de Winter in

The White Moth, **1924.**

The Shooting of Dan McGrew, **1924.**

Thy Name is Woman, 1924.

After a forbidden moment.

Barbara's past is about to catch up to her.

his 1921 swashbuckling epic, *The Three Musketeers,* and her stardom was assured. *The Three Musketeers* was one of the year's best received pictures and La Marr did not pass by the public unnoticed. While Marguerite de la Motte received most of Doug's attention on-screen, it was the satin-haired La Marr who caught the audience's eye. As a result of this one role, First National, Metro and Goldwyn all featured this ravishing beauty on the screen, and as you must have guessed by now, La Marr's problems continued to mount with the rapid ascent of her screen career.

It was not uncommon for young actors and even total strangers to break into her home in the evenings to profess their love and adoration. Some even threatened to immediately kill themselves right on her new white carpet should she fail to respond. Scenes such as these created some embarrassing moments for La Marr, especially when entertaining guests. This sort of adulation was too much and Barbara bought a watchdog especially trained to break up the suitor's histrionic display upon command, sending him flee-

***Heart of a Siren*, 1925.**

ing for his life. History has not recorded that a second performance was given by any young gentleman who once faced the dog.

As if her personal life had not been confused enough, La Marr had the misfortune to marry once more, this time to Jack Daugherty, a handsome juvenile actor whose screen career at Universal would soon flounder in serial roles. After making *The Eternal City*

***The Girl From Montmartre,* 1926.**

in 1923, La Marr was earning thousands; her new husband, whose paycheck was considerably less, soon came to resent not only her success, but the fact that other men just could not keep their eyes off her. These problems developed into a psychopathic jealousy on Daugherty's part, and while this domestic crisis was developing, La Marr also found it necessary to rebuff several attempts at blackmail by former acquaintances who felt that her earlier life would make a profitable and interesting story for the world to read.

To further complicate Barbara's life, there was the problem of Paul Bern. Bern, who was later to marry Harlow, was madly in love with La Marr and soon after she refused his proposal for that of Daugherty, he attempted suicide. Friends assured Barbara that remorse was not Bern's real problem, but she found it difficult to believe that his attempted suicide had been made after her refusal to marry him. By this time, it was difficult for her to separate Raetha Watson from Barbara La Marr; little wonder that she soon took to heavy drinking, squandering her money and neglecting her work.

Insecurities had dogged her every footstep and each tragic turn of events reinforced Barbara's deep-seated feeling that her beauty was indeed a plague. Unfortunately, she adored the attention men lavished upon her and one suspects that she also enjoyed bemoaning the cruel tricks which fate played as a result of this attention. The same insecurities were part of her professional life; not everyone was convinced that La Marr had talent. Her films quite often revolved around the Eternal Triangle, with Barbara playing the "other woman," and the difficult characterizations required sometimes slipped away from her. A few directors, like Arthur Sawyer, tended to emphasize the voluptuous La Marr figure in preference to her acting, but men like Rex Ingram, George Fitzmaurice and Reginald Barker were able to wring good performances from Barbara. While her films were high-calibre productions, with flashy production values, La Marr still felt it necessary to prove her worth by writing poetry (which was published) and original screen plays (which were sold), but as time went on, her grasp on reality grew slimmer. Alcohol, narcotics and tuberculosis combined to send Barbara La Marr into a sanitarium, where she died January 30, 1926. The cause of death? An overdose of beauty.

LILA LEE

Many filmgoers of the 1920s were hard pressed to decide whether Lila Lee was just another pretty face, or a real talent who was being deprived of an opportunity to develop on-screen. Lila came to pictures in ingenue roles but just as her career got well underway, personal problems forced her to leave the screen for a few years. When she did return it was to adult roles, and the transitional period of development was never recorded on film. While her early roles were in well-mounted Paramount productions, the bulk of her later work was done for independents like Gotham, Tiffany and Chesterfield, and this naturally widened the gulf between what she was and what she might have been.

Although Lila worked with some of the silver screen's most glamorous names in her decade and a half before the camera—Valentino (*Blood and Sand*), Houdini (*Terror Island*), Tommy Meighan (*Male and Female*)—her roles were mostly those of the good girl who shared the hero temporarily with Gloria Swanson, Nita Naldi and other sophisticates. But this trim, vivacious bundle of delight should have skipped her way to the very top with ease, yet Lila didn't make enough films to leave us a clearly delineated picture of her talent and of the 42 or so silents in which she appeared, over half were quickies made in the last three years of the silent film's reign. Was she sophisticate, ingenue, flapper or melodramatic heroine? The answer to this question was never really given audiences by the pert little Augusta Apple, born in Union Hill, New Jersey, in 1902.

The darling of her neighborhood, young Lila showed an early tendency toward the world of fancy and made her first professional

LILA LEE

Lila in *The Cruise of the Make-Believes,* 1918.

appearance in vaudeville around 1910 with Gus Edwards, who nicknamed her "Cuddles" and encouraged the youngster to continue with a career by featuring her in several of his "kid" revues. By 1918, Lila had an impressive list of stage credits behind her for her age and Jesse Lasky signed Miss Lee for *The Cruise of the Make-Believes.* This film turned out to be an interesting beginning for a screen career. Lila's forthright and tender portrayal as Maggie caused reviewers to note that while she was not yet a screen actress, her distinctive personality allowed her to unconsciously feel the spirit of the part. Most felt that as long as Lila did not try to be anything other than she was—a little girl with black hair framing a beautiful face—the movie-going public would fall in love with her, provided Paramount continued to supply her with suitable stories.

Paramount signed the 16 year old to a five-year contract, and very soon she was cast with such accomplished artists as Gloria Swanson (*Male and Female*) and Roscoe Arbuckle (*The Dollar a Year Man*). Lila's career certainly looked as though it was all moonlight and roses the rest of the way. But in 1920, she married

James Kirkwood, an actor-producer twice her age (40) and what appeared to be a happy honeymoon turned into tragedy just a month later. Fond of horses, Kirkwood fancied himself quite the athlete, but a fall from the saddle fractured his skull and brought a temporary halt to Lila's ascending star.

For awhile, his life and career hung in the balance, but Kirkwood pulled through, but as a result of the many months he was laid up recuperating, he lost a large production contract. Bills added up and the newlyweds found money problems to be a large worry; Lila's paycheck alone failed to cover them. She worked intermittently, nursing her husband between jobs, and by the mid-twenties, both were in action again. But the majors had no use for Kirkwood and Lila stuck by his side staunchly, starring in whatever roles she could acquire and insisting that her husband produce the film, if at all possible. Thus, many of her later pictures found the two working together.

But other complications had developed. Now there was a James Kirkwood Jr. to care for and the parents gradually discovered that romance had disappeared from their marriage. A separation even-

Lila and Harrison Ford.

With Gloria Swanson and Tom Meighan in de Mille's *Male and Female,* 1919.

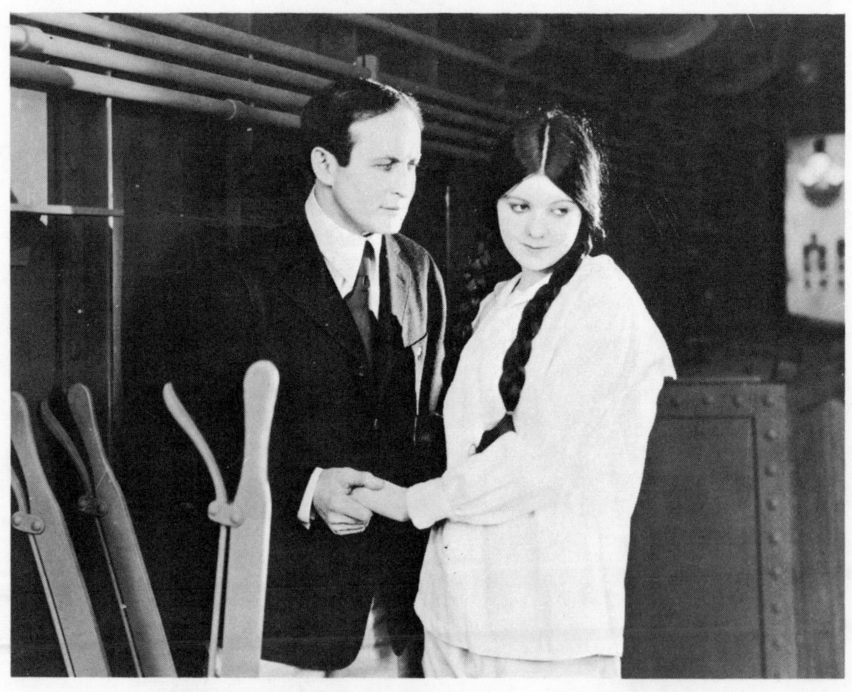

With Harry Houdini in *Terror Island,* 1920.

Lila and Rudolph Valentino in *Blood and Sand,* 1922.

tually took place, with Kirkwood suing for divorce in 1930. Shortly after finishing *Queen of the Night Clubs* for Bryan Foy in 1929, Lila found that she had tuberculosis and a lengthy rest was in order. Once she had recovered, Miss Lee made a series of talkies before leaving Hollywood for a return to New York and roles in the stage hits, *Kiss and Tell* and *Claudia.*

Lila's later pictures had ranged from a feature remake for Rayart of the hoary old Thanhouser serial story, *The Million Dollar Mystery,* to *The Adorable Cheat* for Chesterfield, in which Lila played a rich girl who fell in love with a poor shipping clerk. Doing her best to hide her wealth, Lila's heroine was really a wholesome pseudo-flapper and the petite star's naturalness in the role made *The Adorable Cheat* an appealing picture in spite of its rather misleading title.

Fortunately for Lila, she was not an actress to whom fame and fortune were the end of the world, and over the years she has kept busy with an occasional performance on television, re-

A moment of despair from *Blood and Sand.*

covering from recurring bouts with a variety of illnesses and enjoying life in general. Unlike some of her contemporaries, she's not embittered toward Hollywood or the stardom that might have been, and for that alone, those of us who were her fans are grateful. We just wish that Lila had made more pictures!

BESSIE LOVE

A few of the silent screen's more attractive heroines failed to achieve the great success that had been predicted early in their careers, and no better example comes to mind than the case of Bessie Love. Born Juanita Horton in Midland, Texas, just before the turn of the century, this enchanting little girl had made her first screen appearance as an extra in *The Birth of a Nation* while still in high school. One of that legendary stock company assembled and touched by the directoral magic of D. W. Griffith (who had thoughtfully provided her with the new screen name), Bessie was next seen as "The Bride of Cana" in *Intolerance,* and played a strong supporting role in Triangle's *Acquitted* before carrying the lead with John Emerson in *The Flying Torpedo.* On the strength of these performances and Griffith's recommendation, Bessie was cast opposite William S. Hart in *The Aryan* and came through with flying colors in this classic western, delivering a letter-perfect performance. The role should have boosted the 14-year old youngster into the orbit of continued stardom. But things just didn't meld for her, and by the early twenties Bessie Love was just another leading lady expertly plying her trade, mostly in independent films.

After leaving Griffith, Bessie was given scripts that kept her from projecting a clear-cut image of herself, a circumstance that also happened to other favorite actresses of Griffith. She played too many parts which would have been better suited for Lillian Gish, Mae Marsh and Mary Pickford, and as these three stars had quite differing screen images, it's easy to see how Bessie Love's career got lost in the shuffle. In those few roles that were specifically created to fit her talents, Bessie was just a shade less than superb,

BESSIE LOVE

but no screen actress could maintain a reputation when parts came along so infrequently.

As producers never seemed interested in letting Bessie grow up on-screen, she's best remembered for her "sweet sixteen" portrayals, yet her two most interesting roles of the twenties were quite

With Douglas Fairbanks in *Reggie Mixes In,* 1916.

Arthur Hoyt, Lewis Stone, Wallace Beery, Bessie, and Lloyd Hughes in *The Lost World,* 1925. Bessie's fine performance was lost in the shadows created by Willis H. O'Brien's miniature monsters, who stole the show from the human actors.

Bessie during her Triangle years.

different. As the island dancer in *Soul Fire* with Richard Barthelmess and the girl Mary whose love could not be returned by Adolphe Menjou in *The King on Main Street* (in which Bessie introduced

With Lloyd Hughes in *The Lost World,* 1925.

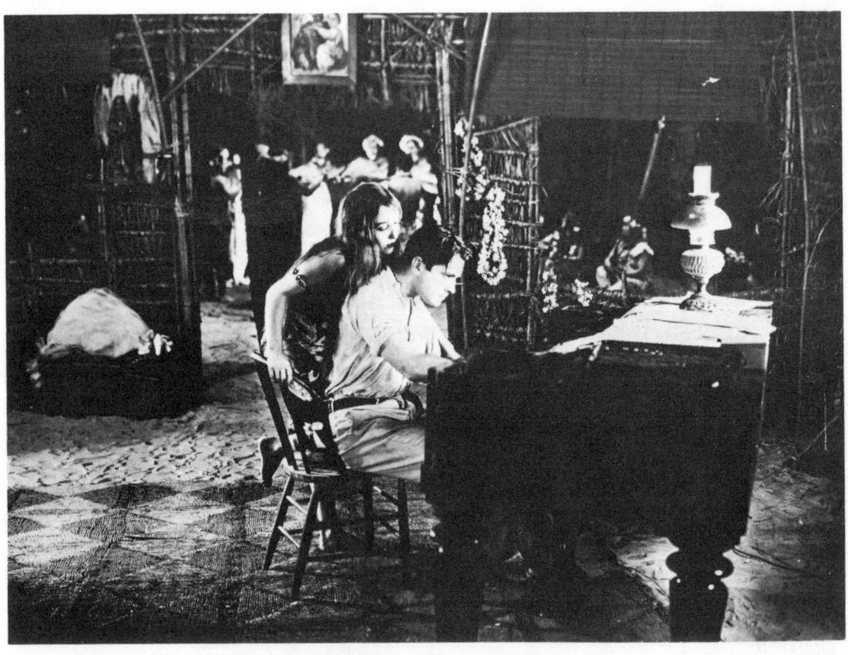

Another fine performance as the island girl in *Soul Fire,* 1925, with Richard Barthelmess.

***Young April,* 1926.**

the Charleston to the screen), her dramatic performances were highly praised. But provocative roles like these proved too rare to sustain top stardom, and while charming little program pictures like *Young April, Lovey Mary* and *Dress Parade* kept her before a fickle public's eye, they did nothing much for her career. Even a box-office hit like *The Lost World* failed to be the plum it should have been; no one went to see the cast perform—the special effects and miniatures of Willis H. O'Brien were the real stars and *The Lost World* was the monsters' movie all the way!

Although the fan magazines continually hailed a choice role as another "comeback" for Bessie, she was soon forgotten again, and the dramatic potential of this fine little actress was mishandled and wasted in film after film. Her last "comeback" was in the industry's first talkie/musical, M-G-M's *The Broadway Melody* (1929) and Bessie found herself in a hit, singing and dancing to the lilting score by Herb Brown and Arthur Freed. This was definitely Bessie Love's year; she married William Hawks and the great box-office success of *The Broadway Melody* led directly to a skit in *The Hollywood Revue.*

The versatile Miss Love had no trouble adapting to the talkies,

As a star-spangled hoofer in *The Broadway Melody,* 1929.

but she retired in 1931 to await the birth of her daughter Patricia the following year. Falling in love with England during a subsequent European tour, Bessie moved to London to live when her marriage dissolved a couple of years later. That was over 35 years ago, and the eternal gamine hasn't stopped working yet. Stage, screen, radio and television roles have come her way with sufficient vigor to keep her from really retiring. A few years ago, her American fans got a real treat when they went to see *Isadora* and found Bessie cast as the mother.

Although in her seventies, the alter ego of little Juanita Horton has not slowed down. In recent years, she discovered that the pen is also a potent performer and Bessie Love, whose specialty was once short stories, now reviews books, contributing criticism and comments on the days of the silent screen for *Sight and Sound* and other cinema periodicals; it almost seems as if Bessie will be with us forever, bless her.

MAE MARSH

The stock company of screen players assembled by D. W. Griffith at Biograph during 1909–12 contained many of the early drama's favorite actresses. It was not unusual to be "discovered" by Griffith, the finest talent seemed to naturally gravitate into his hands, to be molded and shaped as no other director before or after seemed able to do with such ease and consistency. Lillian Gish, Mary Pickford and Blanche Sweet quickly rose to the top of their profession, as did Mae Marsh, who joined Biograph at age 14 and today is regarded by many critics and historians as Griffith's finest contribution to the dramatic screen.

Born Mary Wayne Marsh in Madrid, New Mexico, in 1895, Mae came to Griffith's attention in 1910 while visiting the Biograph western studio to watch her older sister Marguerite at work in front of the camera. Unknown to Mae, Dorothy Bernard brought the director in to watch her and Griffith immediately sensed those certain qualities he looked for in his heroines. As a result, the youthful Mae was invited to become a movie actress during the winter months when Griffith filmed in California. In 1912, she worked for Kalem and Imp briefly before deciding upon a screen career and joining Biograph permanently in New York City. In an interview given years later, Griffith would recall that of all the actresses with whom he had worked, Mae was the only one whose natural talent was sufficient to allow her to reach the top without long, hard hours of training.

Mae's speciality soon became the adolescent heroine suddenly thrust into the realities and responsibilities of adulthood. While she possessed that frail appearance characteristic of the favored

MAE MARSH

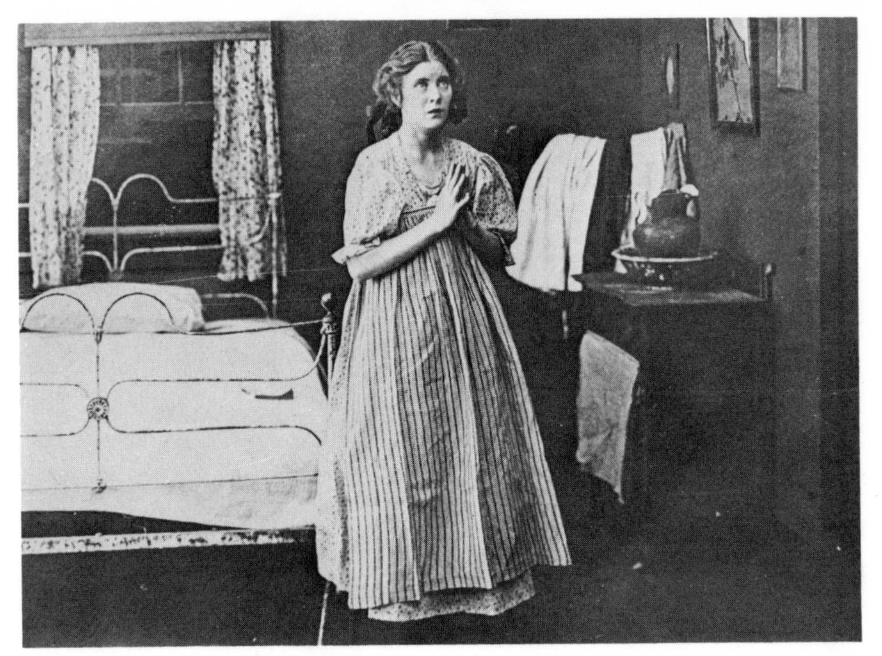

***The Little Liar,* 1916.**

Griffith heroines, an inner strength projected itself on-screen, allowing her to carry off the role transformation with believability. A sad humility, coupled with intense sincerity, became her screen trademark. Mae was used extensively by Griffith in both starring and supporting roles during 1912–13. Making her own costumes and applying her own make-up during that formative period of the screen, Mae steadfastly maintained that her years with Griffith were the really exciting ones in the motion picture's development from a vaudeville "chaser" to a full-fledged artistic medium of expression.

Although she had worked in uncounted Griffith pictures, it was Mae's role as the "Little Sister" in *The Birth of a Nation* that brought her talents into sharp focus. Her welcome of the returning "Little Colonel" home from the war still catches viewers with a lump in their throats, as her happiness turned from a joyous and tender compassion to anxiety-laden sadness at his appearance. Later in the epic, Mae's suicidal leap from a cliff to escape her fate at the hands of an emancipated slave brought audience sympathy firmly on her side.

A year later, she gave yet another superb performance as

The Wharf Rat **(1916), with Robert Harron and Spottiswoode Aitken.**

The Face in the Dark, **1918.**

Robert Harron's grief-stricken wife in the modern sequence of *Intolerance* (some of which had been filmed before *The Birth of a Nation*), which was quite possibly the finest dramatic appearance of the year. She also costarred with Harron in a number of the Griffith-supervised Fine Arts productions for Triangle release, with roles ranging from the romantic *Hoodoo Ann* and *The Wharf Rat* to melodramas like *A Child of the Paris Streets.*

But as was the case with all of Griffith's heroines, Mae eventually left the Master for greener fields, becoming one of Goldwyn's star attractions at $3000 weekly in 1916 (she would earn $250,000 annually before her contract expired), but her career reached a plateau and stalled. No one at Goldwyn seemed to know quite what to do with her. The roles given Mae did not fit her and even her directors seemed equally at a loss as to how best to present her.

To other screen actresses, it would have been an extremely frustrating experience, but Mae's whole life was not dependent upon her screen success. In 1918 she married Louis Arms, a journalist turned Goldwyn publicist. Distrustful of the ballyhoo surrounding the movies, Mae had at first refused to cooperate with Arms while making *Polly of the Circus,* but the enterprising young man (who was soon fired by Goldwyn for promoting Madge Kennedy's *Baby Mine* as the fastest filmed—10 days—feature in movie history) not only gained her cooperation, he married her shortly after the incident.

Mae's marriage meant more to her than a career and after her Goldwyn contract was completed in 1918, she left the screen for two years. Returning in 1920 to work for Robertson-Cole, she then appeared in a few independents and a pair of foreign films before leaving the screen to raise her growing family. In those years following her departure from Fine Arts and Griffith, Mae's single emotional role (and one that pointed out how far superior her talents as an actress had exceeded the material given her by Goldwyn and others) came in a reunion with D. W. Griffith and the lead in his 1923 *The White Rose.* As the young heroine seduced by Ivor Novello, Mae underwent tragedy after tragedy before arriving at the happy ending. This was a part Mae could really bite into and her performance counterbalanced Griffith's tendency toward the mawkish sentimentality that often marred his efforts.

Reappearing in 1931 as Ma Shelby in the Fox remake of *Over the Hill,* Mae's strongly expressive and mature features made her perfect for emotional character parts, and over the next three

***The Beloved Traitor,* 1918.**

decades she was often seen in cameo and bit roles in films ranging from the Doris Day thriller *Julie* to John Ford's *Three Godfathers* and *They Rode Together.* The ultimate tribute was paid Mae Marsh in 1955 when the George Eastman House's Festival of Fine

***The Glorious Adventure,* 1918.**

Arts named her as one of the five outstanding screen actresses of the silent era. Graciously accepting the honor, Mae returned to her husband and home in Hermosa Beach, California, to continue with her occasional screen work, painting and sculpting, until her death in 1968.

Over the years, Mae had been paid many compliments for her fine acting, but she held no regrets about having given up a starring career for her family. The same humility and sincerity which she so adeptly portrayed on the screen characterized her own life. As she once remarked, the glamor of Hollywood as she had known it was a poor substitute for the happiness that three children (and nine grandchildren) had brought her—a commentary on life that marked the essence of Mae Marsh.

MARY MILES MINTER

Under the guise of freedom of the press and the right of the public to know, American newspapers during the early twenties took an almost perverted delight in destroying the screen idols created by their readers' patronage at the box-office over the previous decade. Nickels and dimes had elevated ordinary mortals to the status of superhuman gods and goddesses and placed them on the silver screen in full view of an adoring public. The price for this supreme tribute was a simple one—the stars were required to open their private lives to public view and yet not destroy the illusion by appearing too human. It was a near impossible request—to live the glamorous life of a star without violating the mores of a fundamentalist nation—and not even the onset of the Jazz Age would make it any easier. But while many stars managed to balance their lives on the tightrope treadmill, some failed miserably and others, like Mary Miles Minter, were victims of circumstances.

As 1922 dawned, no young star had a brighter future to look forward to. Only 20 years old, Mary Miles Minter was on the threshold of real screen fame when her career suffered a fatal blow with the death of William Desmond Taylor, her friend and director. Although no solid evidence was ever produced in a court of law which would link Mary with Taylor's death (still an unsolved crime), the press implied the connection with tantalizing hints of monogrammed nightgowns, narcotics and sex. Mary's fans were many by this time and would not have deserted her, had it not been for the influence of yellow journalism at its worst and a frightened studio which had barely finished sacrificing Roscoe Arbuckle on the altar of the muckrakers' public indignation.

MARY MILES MINTER

Born Juliet Reilly in Shreveport, Louisiana, Mary began her stage career at a tender age as Juliet Shelby, and in a few short years she had appeared in well-known plays with some of America's leading stage actors (Nat Goodwin, the Farnum brothers, Robert Hilliard), winning the plaudits of even the most difficult of critics. At the age of ten, she appeared in the 1912 film version of *The*

Mary and her sister Margaret Shelby.

Littlest Rebel for Powers, and two years later she received recognition when the *Dramatic Mirror* reviewed her first starring role in *The Fairy and the Waif,* a Frohman release. Columbia Photoplays, one of the Metro affiliates, signed the budding actress, and in late

***Anne of Green Gables,* 1919.**

summer of 1915 she was billed along with Francis X. Bushman, Olga Petrova and William Faversham as one of Metro's four biggest stars. But Mary's stay on the lot lasted only a short year. Gertrude Shelby, surely the stereotype of all stage mothers, moved her daughter to American for more money than miserly Louis B. Mayer would pay and there Mary remained until 1919.

During this time, she began building an enormous following of fans. When Mary Pickford left Paramount to form United Artists with Chaplin and Fairbanks, Paramount looked around for a blue-eyed blonde whose unsophisticated charm would project in the Pickford fashion. Mary was chosen and signed to a 3½ year contract to appear in Realart pictures, with a minimum guarantee of $1.3 million. But Paramount overlooked one thing—Mary Pickford was Miss Personality, with a depth and range of acting ability, and a long proven box-office appeal that allowed her some approval in her scripts. By comparison, Mary Miles Minter was an unknown whose screen personality needed further development to give it substance.

Sweet Lavender, **1920.**

Nurse Marjorie, **1920.**

***The Heart Specialist,* 1922.**

Although the stories Paramount assigned Mary required little acting ability, they were well-mounted vehicles which allowed her to project a personality that captivated most who saw her. At Realart, Mary Miles Minter began to achieve what many had predicted for her—stardom. Even so, Mary was not at all pleased with the roles given her and longed for more substantial parts, but *Anne*

With Tony Moreno and Ernest Torrence in *The Trail of the Lonesome Pine* (1923), her final screen appearance.

of Green Gables, Judy of Rogue's Harbor and *Jenny Be Good* placed her innocent charms and youthful sunshine on the screen where fans found it difficult to resist this utterly charming child. Paramount even bought Emerson Hough's *The Covered Wagon* as a vehicle for Mary, but she refused to do it (the part eventually went to Lois Wilson) and with Taylor's untimely demise, Mary's career ended in a sensational manner. Few would have foreseen this finale for the demure little girl who worked hard on-set every day, spending quiet evenings at home with her mother, sister and grandmother. Paramount allowed Miss Minter to complete her contract and with the release of her final film (*The Trail of the Lonesome Pine*) in April 1923, Mary Miles Minter was retired from public view.

While few of Mary's films have been seen for years, the recent fashion has been to denigrate her talents in favor of the director, or his personal feelings about working with her, hardly an objective approach. But throughout the years, Miss Minter has remained steadfastly quiet about the past when such articles have appeared in print. Temperamental she may have been, but the question of temperament should not be so easily raised and dropped without considering both her age and relationship with her mother, who pushed, shoved and bent the girl ever in the direction of opportunity, enjoying the rewards of Mary's screen appeal with little concern for her future. The temperament was an extension of her mother, over which Miss Minter had little control. It also probably mirrored Mary's problems with her sister Margaret, who had once coveted a screen career of her own only to fail. Those quiet evenings at home must have been a real test of Mary's inner strength.

Once deposed from the screen, Mary had no money or income and immediately engaged her mother in a bitter debate about her past earnings, an acrimonious matter that the newspapers reported with glee, and one that ended with the establishment of a trust fund in 1924. Eventually turning to interior decorating, Miss Minter ran a successful business, but even her later years were hardly peaceful. A few months before her sister died in 1937, Margaret suddenly turned on her mother, indirectly accusing Mrs. Shelby of withholding information concerning Taylor's murder and leading to a reopening of the entire sordid affair. But the District Attorney's office found no evidence it considered relevant and proclaimed Mrs. Shelby innocent of any wrongdoing.

That such a promising career should have been cut short just when it was beginning to blossom was the public's loss. Although often compared at the time to Mary Pickford, Miss Minter was not as complete an actress as Pickford, or even Gish, but her full potential had hardly been scratched. With maturity, freedom from parental control and sound career management, Mary Miles Minter would have certainly remained a bright star for many more years, leaving us with a much larger and varied legacy of her talent.

MAE MURRAY

To a nation of small towns, Hollywood in the twenties was the epitome of glamor; those of us not fortunate enough to live right in make-believe land vicariously shared life there with the lucky inhabitants through the eyes of numerous syndicated columnists, a profusion of fan magazines and countless evenings spent in a darkened theater. This was the magic of the movie capital, for just below its surface dozens of favorite personalities whom our nickels and dimes had made stars led a life very different from that we imagined. For every Mary Pickford who adjusted reasonably well to the Cinderella world, a Barbara La Marr could be found, with external gaiety masking the internal tragedies. Only human, the stars created their own problems; some just seemed to be less capable of coping with reality than others. No better example of this comes to mind than that of Marie Adrienne Koenig, a pretty little girl from Portsmouth, Virginia, who would come to symbolize the silent screen's glamor to an increasingly restless and mobile nation in search of itself.

Marie's early career closely followed a script written in the best Hollywood tradition and the American Dream; discovered dancing in a small cabaret by songwriter Irving Berlin, she became Irene Castle's temporary replacement in his musical *Watch Your Step* and rightly or not she took credit ever after for saving the show from ruin. Ziegfeld took notice and she leapfrogged from his Follies in 1915 to the motion picture screen, with a helping hand from Jesse Lasky. Now known as Mae Murray, her first screen role was the lead in a potboiler called *To Have and to Hold* (1916), held together mainly by a strong cast which included the popular

MAE MURRAY

***On With the Dance,* 1920.**

Mae in her first screen role, *To Have and to Hold,* 1916.

***Idols of Clay,* 1920.**

Wallace Reid. She was a fine dancer, but her acting was far from convincing; and while a gifted actress might have saved the pieces, Mae hadn't sufficient experience to handle the part. This was followed by *The Dream Girl* and *The Big Sister,* neither of which satisfied Mae and Jesse Lasky. But refusing to give up on her, Lasky hired Robert Z. Leonard, then directing at Universal, to take charge of Mae's screen career.

A one-time actor who had gone behind the camera with some success, Leonard hit it off in grand style with Mae at the outset of their collaboration, which began with *The Plow Girl.* Mae had few pretensions about her acting ability, but she *was* a star and demanded to be treated as one. Leonard made the effort to understand her and their professional bond soon became a personal one as well. But about this time, Mae's temperament and inability to hold herself in check began to take over her career. Her first marriage to William M. Schwenker Jr. in 1908 had ended in divorce, and while filming *The Primrose Path* she married again, this time to an old acquaintance, Jay O'Brien. The ink was hardly dry on the marriage certificate when she filed to have the union dissolved, claiming that her new husband had held a gun in her back during the private civil ceremony.

Earning $1200 a week now, Mae married Bob Leonard once the O'Brien fiasco was settled. Together they made a group of interesting and profitable films which would shortly bring her weekly value up to $10,000. From Paramount, the Leonards organized her own company, and every year, the pace of life grew quicker and merrier, with Mae trying desperately to live up to her reputation as a hard-working, fast-living member of the world's most glamorous profession. *The Mormon Maid, The Restless Sex* and *Circe, The Enchantress* established Mae as a popular favorite and publicity departments ground out miles of copy about "the girl with the bee-stung lips." The pace grew so hectic that Mae and Leonard parted company in 1925.

That same year, the actress went into Metro's *The Merry Widow,* working for a no-nonsense director, Erich Von Stroheim.

***Fashion Row,* 1924.**

***Mademoiselle Midnight,* 1924.**

Mae gave what was undoubtedly her best performance in *The Merry Widow,* but constantly clashed with Von Stroheim, who reserved a special contempt for her. Pyrotechnics were the order of the day, with director and star matching each other every step of the way until management stepped in, patched up the numerous quarrels and hastened the whole affair to a quick conclusion. But

Mae and Tully Marshall in *The Merry Widow,* 1925.

in spite of all its troubles, *The Merry Widow* was a great success and Mae's personal concept of her stardom was strongly reinforced.

The mid-twenties had brought a new vogue into fashion—marriage to a European noble for his prestige value—and had Mae been emotionally capable of seeing beyond the glitter, the tragedy to come might have bypassed her; but reaching into the barrel with zest, Mae plucked out a Prince—David M'divani. Their marriage was one of the high points of the 1926 social season in the movie capital, but it almost immediately turned sour.

Accustomed to having men cater to her, Mae had been overwhelmed by the Prince's charming manners, but once he got her signature on a power of attorney, M'divani took control of Mae's $3 million fortune and turned the manners off. She bore him a son, Koran, and walked out on her M-G-M contract at his insistence that no wife of his should work for a living. Often unhappy in the past with his temperamental star, Louis B. Mayer was

***The Merry Widow,* 1925.**

momentarily crushed, but soon recovered and resolved that Mae would never work again if he could help it. As Mae told it to Jane Ardmore in the 1959 autobiography, *The Self-Enchanted,* the next few years were a living hell, punctuated by work in a few independent films (including a sound remake of her *Peacock*

***The Masked Bride*, 1926.**

Alley) and occasional moments of happiness with her growing son. She still considered herself a star and tried to keep up the pretense as best she could, but the tide was against Mae Murray. Accustomed to lavish living, it was difficult for her to get along without her money, social position and work. After the divorce from M'divani, she eventually lost custody of her son and that seemed to be the body blow. Mae sold her personal possessions and soon went bank-

Mae's half-closed eyes, the bee-sting lips, an empty champagne glass, and diamond bracelet—all symbolic of the stereotyped Jazz Age heroine Mae came to represent.

rupt, but through it all, continued to retain her belief that "once a star, always a star."

But Mae's star had set for good; the appearance of her autobiography in 1959 went almost unnoticed, with Mae claiming to have earned only $1500 in royalties. The Motion Picture Relief Fund took over management of her financial affairs and Mae faded into obscurity again until 1964, when she was found wandering the streets of St. Louis in the belief that she was in New York City. She died a year later, still holding fast to her past. The tragedy of Mae Murray would make a screen story rivaling *Madame X;* forgotten by the generation which had loved her and unknown to their children, she had once held the world in the palm of her hand and yet lost everything. The last three decades of Mae's life were shrouded in the darkness of obscurity and, by Mae's standards, poverty. It's a story to which only Liz Taylor could do justice.

NITA NALDI

Only in the celluloid world of make-believe could it happen—a quiet and reserved Irish colleen finding success as a tempestuous Spanish vamp, a sultry French adventuress and a sensuous Italian temptress. These flights of fancy are rather different worlds from the reality of a New York chorus line, but the accomplishment belongs to Donna Dooley and she managed the masquerade so well even her public was convinced that the deception was real.

Born a New Yorker, Donna was another of the early screen stars educated in a convent. In her case, Donna's great aunt happened to be the Mother Superior and the child was sent off to Fort Lee, New Jersey, at an early age. At that time, Fort Lee was still an active center of movie production and even convent life was unable to completely shelter the little lady from the glamor which surrounded screen acting. In later years, Donna reminisced that her earliest ambition had been a determination to follow in the footsteps of Theda Bara as the ranking screen vamp.

Leaving the convent world far behind her, Donna ventured into modeling, then became a dancer in the chorus line at New York's Winter Garden. Although the hours were long, the pay low, and every male in the audience thought of himself as the world's greatest stage-door romeo, Donna knew that the exposure of the chorus line was a way of being seen by the right people—it had worked for Mae Murray and Marion Davies, and it could work for her.

Donna's observation was correct; her dreams did come true. John Barrymore attended a performance at the Winter Garden in

NITA NALDI

1919, while still casting *Dr. Jekyll and Mr. Hyde* for Paramount release. Spotting Donna in the chorus line, he offered her a role as a Spanish dancer in his upcoming film at $15.00 weekly. The dark-haired Miss Dooley accepted and the creation of Nita Naldi began. With a fine performance by Barrymore, *Dr. Jekyll and Mr. Hyde* proved to be among the screen highlights of 1920, and the role of Theresa, one of Barrymore's deviations from Stevenson's

While Lila Lee has won this time, Nita knows that Valentino will soon be hers.

Rudolph Valentino and Nita Naldi in *Blood and Sand,* 1922.

***The Ten Commandments,* 1924.**

classic novel, provided an excellent showcase for Miss Naldi—offers from other producers began to arrive with regularity.

Nita turned up with a brief part in Harry Houdini's production of *The Man From Beyond,* which took a good story premise and

With Jack Holt in *Don't Call It Love,* 1924.

turned it into an unimaginative script boringly translated to the screen. As Marie Le Grande, she was Dr. Turner's female accomplice in his plot to gain control of Jane Connelly's fortune. While the subtitles told audiences that the chief conspirator had used her services many times in the past, they also hinted at a more involved relationship. Her role was a pivotal point in the story—after gaining the confidence of a man named Duval, she was to discover Houdini's secret.

Her appearance in the film brings curiously mixed reactions today. Nita had not fully undergone the metamorphosis from sweet kid to worldly vamp, which the later use of heavy makeup would complete. She looked for all the world like an apprentice on her first assignment. When Turner brought his friend to be plied with liquor and love for the desired information, Miss Naldi stood around with a quizzical expression, appearing to wonder self-consciously just what came next, hardly the mark of a sophisticated female to whom love was a weapon. When Turner suggested use of the plush love seat, Nita appeared almost relieved and scurried over with Duval to begin her mission. Seen fifty years after it was originally filmed, the sequence is an amusing vignette in an otherwise dull film.

Nita's first well-written part came two years later as Dona Sol in Valentino's *Blood and Sand.* By that time, she had the vamp routine down pat and temporarily stealing the bull fighter from Lila Lee was child's play for her. Her makeup was much better and no audience would have believed her Irish parentage, much less have guessed it themselves. Even Nita got a bit carried away with her publicity, which claimed her to be the daughter of a famed but unnamed Italian diplomat. Maintaining that she had a sister in Spain, little Donna Dooley fell in perfectly with the nonsense peddled in fan magazines of the twenties, and with roles in *The Ten Commandments, Cobra* and *A Sainted Devil,* she became one of the outstanding female heavies of the silent screen.

Seldom sympathetic in nature, Nita's roles usually involved her as the "other woman," a wondrous flight of imagination when seen today. Of course, standards of beauty change as generations change, but Miss Naldi's heavy, full-bodied figure was usually clothed in garments designed to minimize the curves, and as a result she appeared quite chunky. The broad face and heavy eyebrows had a certain tinge of masculinity, and with her slightly slanted eyes, Nita's appearance was best described by her contemporaries as "exotic." Years later, chuckling over the deception, she would ascribe the peculiar eyes to her having squinted under hot lights and large reflectors day after day. She maintained that she and Valentino were both "blind as bats."

Nita Naldi's career as a box-office name lasted less than a decade. Vamping as such went out of style in the late twenties and few practitioners of the art found other screen characterizations with which to extend their careers. Three films with Valentino and a close friendship with his wife Natacha Rambova had helped bolster her brief career, and while it can safely be said that Nita Naldi achieved her early ambition to replace Theda Bara on the screen, her acting talent never extended much beyond a mysterious, inviting look and an ample bosom. She married and went abroad to make a few films, but finally disappeared from the screen. In 1942, Nita turned up as Mistress of Ceremonies at the Diamond Horseshoe's "Silver Screen Revue," an act that required very little on her part. From then until her death on February 17, 1961, she lived in New York, making an occasional return to show business whenever an offer was extended. Probably no Hollywood

With Valentino in *Cobra,* 1926.

personality gave more interviews than Nita Naldi and they were always opinionated, lengthy and spicy—her long friendship with the Valentinos seemed to be her favorite topic. The step from Donna Dooley to Nita Naldi had been a long, hard one and Nita realized that she had Lady Luck and a lot of friends to thank for helping her earn a place in screen history. What more could a girl ask for?

JANE NOVAK

Few silent screen heroines had a busier career than lovely Jane Novak, who seemed to grace the screen monthly during the post-World War I era. Of course, she really didn't, but through 1922, Jane made at least eight films a year, working for any company that would offer her a good role, whether a leading or supporting one. One of Bill Hart's favorite actresses (and one to whom he unsuccessfully proposed), Jane appeared with the big western actor in five of his features and no wonder—the lady was one of the most intensely feminine actresses in the business, yet she could play the outdoor girl without detracting from her femininity. A dependable performer who most often rose above her material (a sad commentary on some of the parts with which she had to work), Jane's ethereal beauty could be almost heavenly at times, especially when she was photographed with soft focus. I've often wondered how she would have projected in a deep role like that of St. Joan, for there was also a quality of inner strength about her which too seldom found an outlet.

Born of middle class parents in St. Louis, Missouri, Jane Novak's very early childhood read like one of the M-G-M musicals of the latter forties—a family of five children and two adoring parents who shared a happy life until her father died quite unexpectedly. Her uncle, owner of the large and successful Theatrical Stock Company in St. Louis, moved in with the Novaks and assumed responsibility for the family's future. Jane was educated at Notre Dame Convent, and when she graduated at 14 she decided to try the stage.

JANE NOVAK

The artificiality of today's young stars, totally manufactured products of an electronic and advertising age, takes the edge from a feat such as Jane and her friend Freida Spitz accomplished—the two girls formed an act, billed themselves as "The Randolph Sisters"

Jane, Mildred June, and Harold Goodwin in *The Rosary*.

and went on the stage. Their parents were not at all pleased when they ran away from home, and so both were shortly brought back and the act broken up, but Jane managed to win her mother's approval to study for the stage. Careers in show business no longer begin in this manner.

Jane's uncle had recently been divorced from Anne Schaefer, an actress then working for Kalem on the West Coast. Miss Schaefer, who had remained good friends with the Novaks, invited her niece for a visit. While Jane had to work hard to convince her mother and uncle that she should go, they eventually approved the trip and the 17 year old girl left for California in 1913. Her first day on the Kalem lot found Jane working in pictures and making the acquaintance of Frank Newburg, whom she would soon marry. For nearly six months she did small roles, mainly in Ruth Roland's pictures, before moving to Vitagraph.

With Vitagraph in 1915, Jane received her first big break when Hal Roach offered her the position of leading lady with his newly formed Rolin Film Company. The novelty of it appealed to Jane, and even though Roach's finances were shaky she made several short films with Roy Stewart and an unknown, Harold C. Lloyd. While Roach was in New York trying to sell his pictures to a distributor, Jane visited Universal City, where she accepted an invitation by Pat Powers to join the Universal forces.

Jane Novak quickly became one of the most sought-after actresses on the Universal lot; everyone wanted her in their pictures and she was given the lead role in *Graft,* a twenty-episode serial which was supposed to make her a star. Unfortunately, *Graft* did not prove to be a popular Universal serial—it was too slow moving and lacked the thrills and spills that serial fans had come to expect from their cliff hangers. But Jane added to her reputation by appearing in the Universal Specials which starred the popular Hobart Bosworth, until she left the screen in 1916 for the birth of her daughter Virginia.

When she was ready to return to work near the end of the year, Jane did not hurry back to Universal but decided instead to free lance and appeared in *The Spirit of '76.* This independent

Robert Gordon and Jane.

Jane and Philippe de Lacy in *Thelma*.

film was withheld from release for many months while its producer was jailed under the sedition laws after a lengthy and well publicized trial. When it was finally distributed in 1919, *The Spirit of '76* did very poorly at the box-office and many wondered what all

Jane, Tully Marshall, and Mary Medina on the set of *Redskin,* her final silent role.

the fuss[1] had been about. Her first work with Hart followed in 1917 with *The Tiger Man* and *Selfish Yates.* While Jane was not bitten by star fever, she refused to be typecast, but it nearly happened. In the early twenties, our heroine undertook several roles in stories of the Northwest and Alaska—*The River's End, The Trail's End, Kazan, Belle of Alaska, The Snow Shoe Trail*—before moving on to her greatest box-office hit, entitled simply *Thelma.* This tender and moving love story of a Norwegian girl in London social circles who returned home vied with her triple characterization in *The Lullaby* as the best role of her career.

By 1925, Jane's sister Eva had entered pictures, winning new fans for the Novaks, and Jane left for England, where she made three pictures (which were not released here until 1926) before returning home. Most of her subsequent work was done for the small independent producers—Columbia, Tiffany, Sterling—and by

1. The film had been considered unpatriotic, as its story held the American Revolution to question. However, the final result was so bad, nobody cared.

Eva Novak

Jane and Eva Novak.

1928, Jane had gradually withdrawn from the screen into a semi-retirement to be with her daughter. *Redskin,* with Richard Dix, was to be her final silent picture and it took both Dix and her old friend and director Victor Schertzinger to persuade her to do the role.

Over the past thirty years, Jane has worked occasionally in talkies when an interesting part came her way, but today she lives in retirement outside Los Angeles, devoting her time to charitable causes. Jane Novak enjoyed a very busy career when she was active and would not have traded the experience for any other. Unlike many stars, she liked her work and was not consumed by the ambition and greed of the Hollywood legend. While little of her screen work is available today, a print of *Thelma* does exist and is worth seeing for too few of the silent stars are represented by their best work. From those of us who remember, our thanks, Jane, for the many entertaining performances you gave us.

OLGA PETROVA

While some readers may express surprise to find Madame Olga Petrova included in this volume, connoisseurs of the early silent film should be delighted, for the all-too-brief screen career of this delightful Polish-born actress has seldom been given sufficient attention to put her stardom in proper perspective. Coming to the screen an international stage favorite, Petrova's beauty combined with her intelligent, sensitive portrayals to make her a favored candidate for a lengthy stardom and Petrova easily conquered the new medium, as she had the stage. But for several small errors of judgment and a dash of bad timing on her part, she could have endured on the screen for many years.

When Milton Collins of Popular Plays and Players contacted her in early 1915; Petrova found it difficult to take him seriously. She had seen very little of the movies and was not particularly impressed by their potential future. Moreover, Petrova did not consider herself qualified for the motion picture. She had worked hard for stage success and failed to see any benefits from a picture career. But a persistent Collins painted a glowing future for her, and much to Petrova's surprise (for she had set her asking price very high), Collins not only readily agreed to the salary, but also to her numerous other stipulations. Almost before the actress realized it, she was under contract and enroute from Chicago to Popular's New York City studio to make her debut before the silent camera.

Petrova made *The Tigress, The Heart of a Painted Woman* and *My Madonna* in quick succession, completing her contract. Popular Plays had recently moved its release from the near-bankrupt

Olga Petrova and Thomas Holding.

Alco to the newly formed Metro, and under Louis B. Mayer's aggressive marketing, the Petrova pictures played a heavy booking schedule which proved them moneymakers. When Popular Plays approached their new star to sign another contract, she demanded and received approval rights on stories, director, cast and sets, in addition to an even more lucrative financial arrangement.

Petrova's first three pictures were directed by Alice Blache, one of the pioneer woman directors, and leaned heavily in the direction of the melodramatic, dependent heroines so much in vogue at the time. But her intense personal magnetism projected with an ease seldom seen in silent drama of the period and helped overcome the artificiality of the roles she was given. Her pictures were to continue in this vein until after filming was completed on *The Black Butterfly,* her tenth screen appearance. At this point in her new career, Petrova decided that the only way to satisfy her desire for what she considered good stories would be to write them herself. So this multi-talented lady took up pen and paper to create heroines more to her own liking–independent and self-sufficient in their dealings with men and the world around them. *Bridges*

Burned, The Soul of a Magdalene, To the Death and *The Waiting Soul* resulted.

Petrova's contract expired in 1917 and she had signed with Jesse Lasky when the first problem arose in her screen career. Popular Plays' New York studio was destroyed by fire, and with it the negatives of her final five unreleased pictures. The company prevailed upon her good graces to remake all five to save it from total ruin; not knowing that the fire loss had been covered by insurance, Petrova agreed and the films were all reshot in five short weeks. This turned out to be a mistake, for Popular Plays did not release these hastily refilmed features at once, but used them in competition with her work for Lasky and Superpictures.

Petrova made three pictures for Lasky—*The Undying Flame, Exile* and *The Law of the Land.* All were directed by Maurice Tourneur and, while clearly his pictures, the relationship between director and star became so tense that Tourneur would not work with her in a fourth effort. But Petrova was busy forming her own company, and in the next two years she made her final five

With Thomas Holding in *Daughter of Destiny,* 1918.

screen appearances, the last of which was *The Panther Woman,* one of her best roles and Petrova's personal favorite.

Taken from the novel *Patience Sparhawk, The Panther Woman* found Madame Petrova as Patience, the daughter of a recently widowed New Englander who moved west and married a dance hall girl. After her father died, Patience went back East, marrying Beverly Peale (Vernon Steele) who soon died from a lethal dose of poison. Tried for his murder, she was convicted and faced the death sentence, which she managed to avoid only at the last moment. The role was that of a typical Petrova heroine—she fought the world with her wits and won.

With this film, Petrova called it quits. Beautiful, talented, a sensitive and intelligent performer, Olga Petrova's heroines were cut from the same cloth as those of Geraldine Farrar and Pauline Frederick. Phrases such as "primal emotion," "smouldering fires" and "true tragedienne" were used by contemporary writers to describe the work of all three. Often described as being a temperamental star, Petrova had engaged the production power head-on to force her interpretation to the screen and proved her point—now money alone could not keep her on the screen. She returned to a triumphant tour of the stage, adding lectures, personal appearances and writing to her busy schedule, financially secure enough to retire in the mid-twenties to pursue her own interests. With her play writing and poetry, Petrova has lived a long and creative life, but one cannot avoid speculating that had she remained on the screen, Madame Olga Petrova might have easily remained one of the top dramatic stars of the twenties and even the thirties.

MARY PICKFORD

Mary Pickford may not have been the screen's greatest actress (she wasn't) but certainly it is fair to say that Mary possessed immense talent (she did) and that she was the most popular lady to grace the screen for two decades (she was). Winning the hearts of nickelodeon audiences in those dark, dim days of the early screen when cast names were still unknown, "Little Mary" held their affections firmly through a lengthy succession of teenage screen adventures which lasted well into her thirties, an acting accomplishment by itself. But Mary was more than just an extremely accomplished performer; she was also a shrewd businesswoman who knew how to maximize her own potential. Almost before the screen was out of its infancy, Mary Pickford was on her way to becoming both an institution and a power with which to reckon in the new industry.

Born Gladys Smith in Toronto, Mary had hit the boards at an early age to help support her family after her father died. A precocious performer with a natural bent for make-believe, she quickly earned the professional respect of the many older actors with whom she worked. Sister Lottie and brother Jack followed her footsteps and the Smith family might well have had a long career in the theatre had not circumstances dictated abandoning it for the steady employment of motion pictures. Mary's screen debut came at age 16 in 1909 with Biograph, and in only a few months she became one of Griffith's most valuable discoveries. But while Griffith treated his actresses as secondary to the stories, Mary saw it differently and resisted his desired interpretation of her roles, giving restrained, natural performances instead, which quickly drew public attention her way.

MARY PICKFORD

The long golden curls and her spontaneity of expression gave Mary an attractive screen personality; her interest, enthusiasm and a competitive spirit merged into a screen presence which the majority of her contemporaries lacked. In addition, the Biograph films of this era were far more professional than those of their competi-

With Mack Sennett at Biograph, 1909.

tors, both from a technical and content standpoint. Thus Mary was shown to good advantage.

While working and learning from the most creative director of the times, Mary absorbed everything about her new occupation with which she came into contact, gradually acquiring her own definite ideas about making films. In later years, Mary's ability to direct, coupled with her concern for proper lighting and photography, were to become important elements in her career, contributing immensely to her continuing success. This in spite of the fact that she had never really believed in those early days that the screen was more than a passing phase in her career as an actress—surely the "shadow pictures" would never last!

Leaving Biograph briefly for Imp and Majestic (and more money), Mary became disenchanted in a very short time, returning to Biograph and Griffith until the lead role in David Belasco's stage production of *A Good Little Devil* came along. It remained for Adolph Zukor to bring Mary back to pictures by buying the rights to film the play and hiring Mary as its star. But it was her *Tess of the Storm Country* that brought Mary Pickford to real prominence, and by 1916 Zukor was paying her half a million dollars yearly and

***The Little American,* 1917.**

***Heart O' the Hills,* 1919.**

***Suds,* 1920.**

Mary had no real desire to return to the stage. A few years later, Zukor would offer her even more *not* to make pictures!

She appeared in a great many pictures for Zukor, alternating between whimsical comedy and deep drama with no apparent great effort. The period 1917–18 proved to be Mary's most prolific and versatile years, with some of the best of the Pickford films (*A Poor*

Little Rich Girl, Rebecca of Sunnybrook Farm, Stella Maris—all quite different in tenor) making their appearance. But Zukor's promise to give Mary a greater voice in her career did not materialize and so 1919 found her at First National, where she did three pictures of which *Daddy Long Legs* was the best.

Over the years, one particular misimpression has grown up around Mary's career—that she always played young innocent girl roles. Yet when catalogued, her career shows itself to be a kind of triangle. At the beginning of her career, Griffith gave Mary a greater range of portrayals at Biograph than she was ever to again enjoy. It was while she worked for Zukor's Famous Players that Mary hit upon the famous characterization, some five years and well over a hundred films after she first appeared on the screen. But by the time she took over direction of her career in 1919, Mary's popularity was quite firmly rooted to variations of the little girl character, at least in the minds of her fans. Yet, some of her finest acting was done out of character.

As one of the co-founders of United Artists (with Charlie

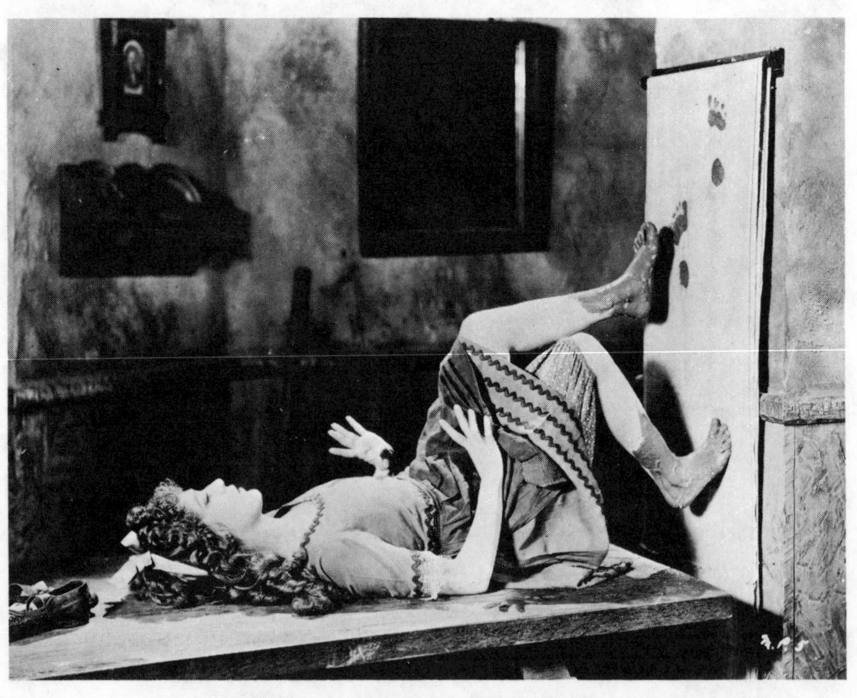

***Through the Back Door,* 1921.**

With Daniel Frohman and Doug Fairbanks.

Chaplin, D. W. Griffith and Douglas Fairbanks) in 1919, Mary at last gained complete control of her own destiny, but wisely did not break drastically with her established screen image immediately. Maintaining the adolescent characters which she portrayed so well, while avoiding the assembly-line appearance one would expect, Mary interspersed them with attempts at adult roles in *The Love Light, Rosita* and *Dorothy Vernon of Haddon Hall.* She returned

***Rosita,* 1923.**

***Dorothy Vernon of Haddon Hall,* 1924.**

Little Annie Rooney, 1925.

My Best Girl, 1927, with Charles "Buddy" Rogers, who became her third husband a decade later.

The Taming of the Shrew, 1929.

to form when she discovered that her public preferred the other Mary Pickford, the little girl in curls with whom they felt more comfortable. By then, Mary was making but one picture a year and *Little Annie Rooney, Sparrows* and *My Best Girl* closed out her career in the silents. Three talkies followed, but with *Secrets* in 1933, Mary realized that audience identification with her screen character had become too strong to break and "America's Sweetheart" retired gracefully to private life.

Mary Pickford's popularity was tremendous in the twenties, and for today's generation—which seems to have lost interest in the Hollywood approach to entertainment—it may all be a bit difficult to fathom. But an entire nation was stunned when its idol wed Doug Fairbanks in 1920. The public reception which the newlyweds received when they went abroad that same year was one usually reserved for heads of state, a glimpse of their home at Pickfair became a must for Hollywood tourists and when Mary finally dispensed with the golden curls for a bobbed hairdo, public criticism overwhelmed her. But she made millions, influenced an industry, married three times and never lost faith with her public, quite an achievement for the little girl who had once informed David Belasco that, as the "father" of her family, she must be a success before she was twenty!

While many of Mary Pickford's short films for Biograph, Imp and Majestic seem to have been lost over the years, major archives around the world have preserved a larger and more representative selection of her features than of any other silent screen actress and a study of her career is not as difficult as it might otherwise have been. As for Miss Pickford herself, she has often expressed a dislike for her own films, claiming that she had not made any which pleased her in their entirety, and once planned to purchase those in existence and touch a match to the whole lot. Fortunately, she never carried this out and for those who wish to take the trouble, the many facets of this most popular screen actress of all time can be seen as they were first revealed so long ago. Perhaps with the increasing interest in the silent era, the near future will see some of her features made available to the home collectors' market and the reader will then be able to enjoy Mary Pickford on his own screen. Let's hope so, as no artist whose works are available should be denied from an appreciative public. And Mary's films were so rich with talent that words are highly inadequate substitutes for the celluloid images.

ARLINE PRETTY

During the quarter century before the movies learned to talk, several hundred screen heroines paraded their talents before the camera for our approval. While their number had necessarily started as a small group, the motion picture's immense and growing popularity, as the century's first decade passed into its second, created a great demand for actresses. To be a movie star became the fondest dream of the adolescent generation of that era. Even those past the age of daydreaming occasionally felt a twinge of desire, but fortunately equipped with the wisdom of age, tempered with but a modicum of ambition and lacking talent in that direction, most of the population was content to sit by and watch the younger generation, applauding those who struck a particular chord within when they appeared on screen. All of the screen heroines were successful in that they achieved their goal of becoming actresses, but as in any walk of life, a few proved to be outstanding in terms of talent, popularity or personal appearance and rose above the others to become stars, with all of the attendant fame and fortune which glorified their status.

In the independent production arena especially, the life of a screen heroine was often short and more often precarious. Many disappeared after a few films; some to reappear in supporting and character roles, while the remainder sought a new niche in life.

Volumes have been written trying to define the essence of that magic which led to stardom but I'm more concerned with those between the top stars and the dropout; there were many actresses whose careers were lengthy and reasonably lucrative. For them, work was steady, and while few achieved any spectacular success,

ARLINE PRETTY

each had her own group of loyal fans who made any picture in which she appeared a financial success. These were most often actresses in the truest sense of the word—competent professionals like Bessie Barriscale, Florence Vidor and Arline Pretty, whose performances were so natural and believable that they carried a picture easily, turning in one good performance after another, whether in comedies or dramas. And that was exactly the reason that star dust never elevated them to the status enjoyed by a select few. Of course, some made unwise choices at critical points in their careers, others were victims of accidents, illnesses or alcohol and some simply found themselves accepting too many roles in lesser pictures which were not widely exhibited. While a few were typecast to fame, many found that the same treatment was a ticket to obscurity.

But regardless of the eventual outcome of their careers, the silent screen could not have existed, earned the huge sums of money and continued to grow without the services of these versatile actresses. To them, in large measure, goes the credit for the development of a crude amusement, once deemed worthy only of darkened stores and the discouragement of vaudeville patrons from sitting through more than one show, into an entertainment industry second to none in the world. I've always felt that those who disparage the so-called "B picture" were unable to grasp the understanding that this concept was the "bread and butter" product which allowed producers to experiment and occasionally bring forth *The Birth of a Nation, Ben Hur, The Big Parade* and others which have become outstanding examples of the cinema at its best.

Arline Pretty (her real name) was characteristic of this group of actresses. A Washington, D.C., girl, Arline joined the Columbia Players after completing her education, entering movies in 1913 to support King Baggot at Universal. Her first taste of the limelight came at Vitagraph in 1916–17 and climaxed with the feminine lead in *The Secret Kingdom,* a Graustarkian romantic serial which alternated between the mythical kingdom and the American West. The next few years found the pretty Arline continuing to deliver de-

With Fred Jones in *The Woman in Grey,* 1920.

Arline and Henry G. Sell. Her long career did not place her among the leading stars, and the movies' dependence upon actresses like Miss Pretty is seldom fully appreciated. Here we pay tribute.

pendable performances for a great variety of producers, but remaining virtually unknown all the while.

A high point of her career came in 1920 with the Serico serial, *The Woman in Grey*. While not a particularly noteworthy chapter play from the average serial fan's point of view, *The Woman in Grey* was an outstanding example of a strong plot coupled with action (serials usually had one or the other) and the surviving episodes hold up rather well today. Arline turned in a solid job of acting but the independent serial, like most of her other pictures, did not make her an overnight sensation.

Arline Pretty earned good money, invested it wisely and remains her charming self today. A few years ago, I used a frame enlargement from *The Woman in Grey* on the dust jacket of *Continued Next Week,* my survey of the silent serial, and shortly after, she began to receive fan mail—forty years after it had stopped. Arline found it difficult to believe that so many people who still remembered her would take the time to write. She gratefully and graciously answered all the letters. Over the years, her sight had progressively grown worse, but just recently she underwent an eye operation from which she is recovering as this is written. Her fans will be pleased to know that Arline now faces a brighter future and join with me, I'm sure, in thanking this lovely lady for many fond memories of a childhood long since departed.

AILEEN PRINGLE

Aileen Pringle's stardom was a short-lived romantic affair with a public eager to be titillated by the more exotic ways of love and a bit embarrassed about the whole thing. The daughter of George W. Bisbee, wealthy president of San Francisco's giant Pioneer Fruit Company, Aileen had first appeared on stage in London and then was seen on the New York stage with George Arliss in *The Green Goddess.* Her move to Hollywood and pictures in 1922 ended her marriage to Sir George Pringle. Aileen's first screen role was in *The Sport of Kings.* Soon she was deeply involved in a career rapidly going nowhere in particular when Elinor Glyn arrived on the scene and rescued her from obscurity.

The British authoress of several best-selling romantic novels, Madame Glyn had made quite an impression in Hollywood, attaching herself first to Gloria Swanson and then Clara Bow, whose appearance in *It* meant stardom for the attractive redhead. Actually, Elinor Glyn's writings were relics of a dead past; remnants of the prewar European aristocratic society which had dissipated itself in The Great War. But the Englishwoman was clever enough to realize that the colonies had always been behind the British Empire in its fashions and follies. Regardless of American insistence upon equality and democracy, we were still human enough to hold a romantic awe for titles, nobility and the luxurious life which accompanied both.

While Madame Glyn's biggest successes had preceded the 1914 conflagration, which ultimately stripped European nobility of its *raison d'être* and potency, she shrewdly sold Hollywood a bill of goods, and in the twenties both Metro and Paramount filmed her

AILEEN PRINGLE

works, with the ubiquitous Madame running the show on both lots and aggravating everyone involved. In spite of all the high-sounding verbiage that uttered from Madame Glyn's lips in interview after interview, she was simply selling *sex* (renamed *It*) to a staid society willing to accept the commodity in the guise of Ruritanian romance.

Madame Glyn came into Miss Pringle's life bearing the leading

Conrad Nagel and Aileen in Elinor Glyn's *Three Weeks,* 1924.

With John Gilbert in *His Hour,* another of Madame Glyn's consuming romances.

role in a screen version of her masterpiece, *Three Weeks.* There was a rather striking similarity in appearance between these two women despite their thirty-year difference in age, and surely the authoress took this into consideration before her announcement that Aileen would star in this latest "Elinor Glyn Production." Along with the announcement came a dash of proper publicity; overnight, Aileen Pringle became the daughter of Jamaica's British governor. Urbane, witty and well-educated, Aileen carried off the deception with ease (she and her husband had been residents of the island) and was accepted by one and all as the genuine aristocrat she would soon portray on the screen.

The story of *Three Weeks* was ridiculously simple. Its plot depicted the loveless queen who spent three weeks in reckless abandon with a young British aristocrat before dutifully returning to her throne. The book was a minute-by-minute account of those 21 days filled with stolen passion, with much of the time spent on tiger skins and beds of roses. Such staging was easy to duplicate on screen. The antics of the two lovers proved to be something else, and as a result the lavishly mounted film proved to be rather slow-moving and somewhat of a bore.

But while critics causticly proclaimed it as being superior to the book, *Three Weeks* grossed a large fortune as fans flocked in large numbers to enjoy vicariously its forbidden rapture. Mack Sennett wrote the final chapter to it with a delicious parody starring that mad lover Ben Turpin in *Three Weeks and a Half.* Aileen was lovely as the Queen and Conrad Nagel's career took a giant step (some said forward, others disagreed). But unfortunately for Miss Pringle, this one picture typed her for much of her starring career and she spent breathless moment after breathless moment panting on other tiger skins (at $250 weekly) in films like *His Hour* (with up-and-coming lover John Gilbert) and *Adam and Evil.*

It was the Theda Bara vamp in Freudian disguise—the respectable woman whose unfulfilled love life drove her near-crazy with desire and to whom a few moments of secret indiscretion (always more satisfying to share on the screen than in real life) justified her stepping beyond the bounds of marriage. Madame Glyn could not have chosen a time more appropriate to appear on the scene than during the early twenties of an America undergoing a morality revolution. By 1930, depression audiences were no longer interested in her or her books. Attitudes of love and marriage had moved far beyond her and audiences were caught up with the problems of

***Adam and Evil,* 1927.**

realistic, modern heroines (who also stepped out on the side).

Aileen's career slowly declined with the changing times, and as parts became fewer and further apart she gradually became Hollywood's unofficial delegate and booster. Years later, she would ironically remark that whenever M-G-M signed a new author, she was always on hand at the station for his arrival. Hardly an important star of the silent screen, Aileen *was* symbolic of the glamor that surrounded those golden years of the movies, a feat accomplished in large measure by the single role for which she is remembered today.

ALLENE RAY

When Pearl White's Pathé contract expired in 1919, she moved over to Fox and a series of feature pictures. Pearl had quit the chapter plays at the peak of her popularity and Pathé executives began a frantic search for another blonde capable of assuming her mantle as "The Serial Queen." In 1917, Pathé had started to groom petite Mollie King in serial roles, but Molly decided that she really didn't want to be another Miss White. Late in 1919, Juanita Hansen was signed and just as the big push toward stardom got underway, Juanita's narcotics addiction was discovered. Fearful of the adverse publicity should the news break out, and unaccustomed to production delays while an incapacitated heroine sobered up, Pathé let Miss Hansen go after completing her second role.

Their search for a wholesome, All-American actress ended in 1924 with the acquisition of Allene Burch, a San Antonio, Texas girl. While her acting credentials were limited, Allene's beauty had won several competitions, including the *Motion Picture Classic*'s "Fame and Fortune" contest. Allene had entered films in 1919 when Harry Myers brought his independent production unit to San Antonio to film a series of westerns. He picked Allene as his leading lady, changing her name to Ray. The Myers-Ray westerns were not profound, as horse operas went. However Allene was an outdoor girl who appeared equally at home dressed in silk and satin.

Pathé's concept of the serial had undergone a substantial revision in the early twenties. The Pearl White cliffhangers had placed their major emphasis on Pearl's self-sufficiency, playing down the romantic angle. But censorship attempts and the changing tastes of twenties' audiences dictated a complete reversal of the formula, and

Contemplating her fate in *The Fortieth Door,* 1924. Allene's blonde tresses were hidden beneath a black wig for this serial.

Allene became the romantically inclined heroine who could take care of herself, but only to a point. This created a need for a strong masculine symbol upon whom she could rely. Allene's first four serials featured Harold Miller, Jack Mower, Johnnie Walker and Bruce Gordon as her leading men, but none really filled the bill.

Chapter play peril from *The Fortieth Door,* 1924.

The symbol eventually appeared in the person of Walter Miller (whose career dated back to the early days of Biograph) and the team of Miller and Ray became the serial screen's personification of the red-blooded, All-American boy and girl during the twenties.

Although she hit it off immediately with fans at the box-office, Allene's first few appearances in front of the serial camera had not been terribly exciting moments. She needed direction and lots of it to run the emotional gamut required of a serial actress in each episode. With the patient, sure hand of director George B. Seitz guiding her, Allene quickly achieved the minimum variety of expression necessary. Beginning with *Sunken Silver* (her fifth serial), Miller and Ray were destined to appear in nine more chapter plays before the silent era (and Miss Ray's career) ended.

Many of her scripts were written by Frank Leon Smith, the dean of serial writers and an old hand at incorporating intrigue, pathos and humor in a well-balanced story. In fact, probably the slickest serial to come out of the silent period was *The Green Archer,* a Miller-Ray epic directed by Spencer G. Bennet, who took

With Walter Miller and Willie Fung in *The Black Book,* 1929, Pathé's final serial.

Seitz's place in 1925 as the ranking Pathé serial director. Bennet recalls that working with Allene was a pleasure, as she was completely willing to undergo whatever hardships the script called for. Never once did she exhibit the temperament so common to stars, even in the serial realm.

Bennet was a fast worker and with the capable Smith turning out top-notch scripts, the two placed hit after hit on the screen featuring Allene and Walter Miller—*The Green Archer, Snowed In, House Without a Key.* Her supporting casts included villain Frank Lackteen and were the best (and most experienced) in the cliffhanger business; production values were far above the average serial. While Pearl White had once earned $3000 weekly appearing in Pathé serials, Allene's salary never went beyond $500. She was worth much more and Pathé knew it, but in the early twenties, the front office had decided to hold its salary scale down as low as possible and put the extra money into good scripts and well-produced serials. While none of Allene's chapter plays exceeded $90,000 in cost, or about the same amount which Universal spent on its serials at the time, the difference on the screen was immediately apparent. As a result, Allene Ray was the only Serial Queen created in the twenties and a fitting updated successor to Miss White's old title, *The Lady Daredevil of the Films.*

Born of the serials, Allene's career came to a close when the silent serial died. She worked into 1929 with Pathé, appearing in its final chapter play (*The Black Book*) and then moved over to Universal to join Tim McCoy in the very last silent serial, *The Indians Are Coming,* which also happened to be the first of the talking cliffhangers. The script was fashioned to showcase McCoy and Allene's role was fairly simple—smile sweetly, keep the dialogue to a minimum and occasionally look frightened. This type of part was not suited for the athletic Serial Queen, who had done many of her own stunts with her double watching. After a few brief and unsatisfactory feature roles in the early talkies, Allene retired from the movies completely, disappearing into oblivion. A concentrated search a few years ago by myself and Spencer Bennet failed to locate her whereabouts and should Allene Ray happen to read this, I do hope she'll get in touch with me—Spencer and I would certainly enjoy recalling the past with her.

MARIN SAIS

It is strange and sad that so many of the movies' heroines have become almost studies in obscurity, especially when their acting careers date back almost to the very beginning of the silent screen. Born in San Rafael, California, in 1890, Marin had entered pictures with Vitagraph's Brooklyn studio in 1909, and a year later moved to Kalem. There she joined Alice Joyce and Helen Gibson to become one of Kalem's top three female stars during 1910–17. Appearing weekly in innumerable short subjects, Marin was often seen as the female foil for the comic antics of Lloyd Hamilton and Bud Duncan (Ham & Bud). She also did tragedy and melodrama, for versatility played a large role in an actress's success in those very early days, and week after week Marin fought for the honor of womanhood, winning quite handily. When you analyze the few of her films remaining from that period, Marin's relaxed and natural acting comes through strongly in comparison to that of many of her contemporaries, and in addition, the lady was most attractive.

Marin's real fame began in late 1914 when she and Ollie Kirkby made the first of a number of "series" for Kalem. The serial concept had hit the screen with Selig's 1913 *The Adventures of Kathlyn,* but it was Pathé's *The Perils of Pauline* which set off the explosion in chapter play stories. Edison and Kalem, both pioneer producers, were leery of investing the time and money required to develop and produce a good "Continued-Next-Week" story; it was much simpler and less expensive to use the series technique—a continuing character in a group of complete but unrelated stories. While the serial concept required that chapters be exhibited accord-

MARIN SAIS

A dramatic moment from *The Pitfall* (1915), with Tom Lingham.

ing to sequence for story continuity, the exhibitor was free to use any or all of a series in whatever way he chose. Audiences were also fond of the series—there was no waiting until next week for the denouement, and missing one or two installments did not spoil the story. The proof of their popularity is best demonstrated by the 119 episodes of *The Hazards of Helen,* an early railroading series which Kalem began in the fall of 1914.

Kalem made *Stingaree, The Further Adventures of Stingaree, The Social Pirates, The Girl from Frisco, The American Girl* and others with Marin, who usually shared billing honors with Ollie Kirkby. Most segments utilized the same hackneyed plots rewarmed in a different context, requiring a most effective heroine to keep the tame stories moving. Marin Sais was equal to the challenge and contemporary reviewers often panned the plot while praising Miss Sais. She quickly became one of the most often seen and best-remembered of the pre-war screen heroines. But Kalem closed its doors in 1917. A few of its stars had graduated to greater fame with other major companies (most notably, Ruth Roland, Alice Joyce and Carlyle Blackwell), but most of the player roster faded into independent productions where they soon were seen only in character roles and supporting parts. Ollie Kirkby virtually disappeared from the screen and Miss Sais did nothing of real importance until 1920, when she appeared with Jack Hoxie in a western serial, *Thunderbolt Jack.*

Marin had often acted with Hoxie at Kalem back in the early days when she was a star and he was still an extra working under the name of Hart Hoxie. Over the years, the two became very good friends; so good in fact that when Jack's divorce was granted in 1920, he and Marin were married. During the early twenties, they worked together with fair success in a number of independent westerns produced by Ben Wilson. When Jack landed a contract with Universal, he was given other leading ladies and Marin remained in the independent horse operas; the large number of state right westerns produced in the twenties meant that cowgirls were always

True Boardman and Marin.

Tom Lingham and Marin in "A Voice in the Wilderness," chapter 2 of *Stingaree,* 1915.

Tom Lingham, Ollie Kirkby, and Marin in "The Honor of the Road," chapter 7 of *Stingaree,* 1916.

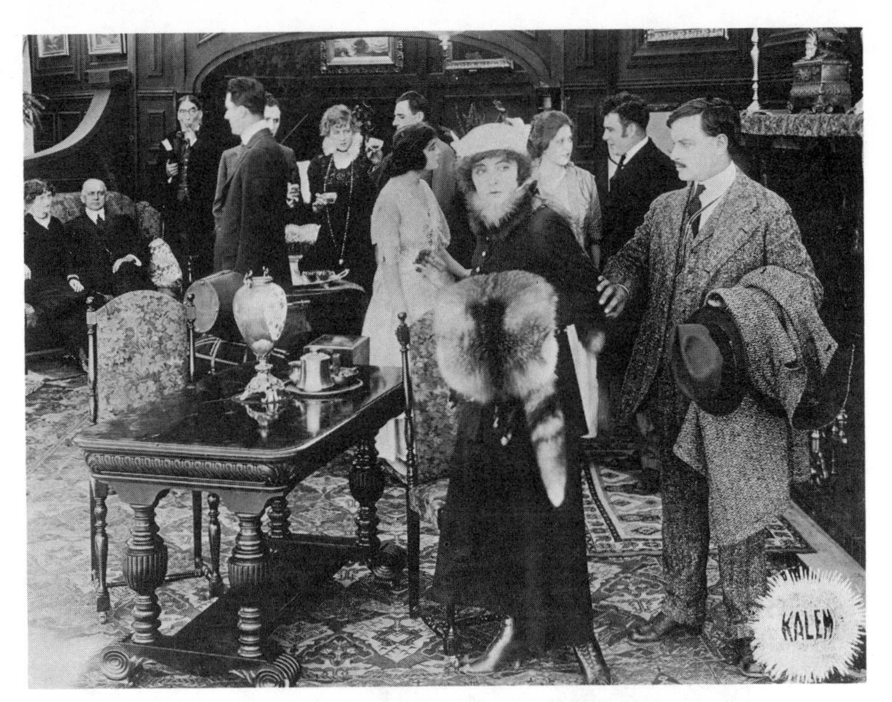

The Darkest Hour, 1916.

On the set of *Stingaree* (1916), with True Boardman, Paul Hurst, Ollie Kirkby, and director James Horne.

Marin Sais in *The Social Pirates.*

in demand. Although Miss Sais was an excellent rider who didn't mind stunting, she was seen less and less in leading roles. By the time sound arrived on the scene late in the decade, Marin's star had faded. After 1925, she and Jack were divorced and her career had settled into a string of secondary and character roles.

***The Social Pirates'* production company.**

Western fans of the late thirties and forties recall Marin Sais best for two roles: she was Calamity Jane in *Deadwood Dick,* and the tough but tender-hearted redhead "Duchess" in the Jim Bannon "Red Ryder" series. By this time, Marin's early career and stardom was unknown to the new generation of audiences, but it's quite unlikely that her past would have made much difference even had they realized that the leathery little old lady had once been a famous star herself; stardom doesn't cut much ice with kids on a Saturday afternoon in a darkened theater.

As for Marin, she stayed in the business just as long as her health would permit it, even though the roles grew smaller and further apart, and then she retired to managing a small apartment house in Hollywood. After her second husband, Arthur Turcott, died she became somewhat of a recluse. Many who tried to look her up while in town had to content themselves with standing on the front steps and gazing at the name above the door bell; the slightest

As star of *The American Girl* series in 1917.

On location for one of *The American Girl* series, director Horne explains an upcoming scene to Marin and Paul Hurst.

suspicion that her caller was other than a prospective tenant or known friend brought silence from the other side of the door. A half-century after her star reached its peak, Marin Sais passed away in the obscurity which she had drawn around her later years, an unfamiliar name from an era virtually forgotten by all but the faithful.

NORMA SHEARER

In the twenties, stardom on the silent screen was a dream in which thousands of young ladies indulged themselves upon retiring each evening and a fair percentage of those who set out to make the dream come true found only bitter disappointment at the end of a long, hard road; a road which often included stops at drama schools established to purposely fleece the gullible would-be actresses on an assembly-line basis. Few were able to start in the business without experience and reach a theatre marquee as did Colleen Moore and Norma Shearer.

A Canadian girl, Norma harbored ambitions of a show business career from her first recollections and had a fair start as a pianist when her father's business failed in Montreal and she found it necessary to go to work. Selling the piano for their fare, Norma and her sister arrived in New York City (with her mother along as chaperone) to begin a career in films. The next few years were spent in near-anonymity, although she did land occasional work in pictures, mainly independents like *The Flapper* and *The Trail of the Law.* To piece out the budget between such jobs, Norma turned to photographic modeling. Ironically, her face graced the countryside as Miss Lotta Miles, a coast-to-coast billboard advertising campaign for Kelly-Springfield tires.

In 1923, her agent Edward Small received a call from the Louis B. Mayer studio asking for a quiet, refined type and he did such a fine selling job over the long distance wire that she received a six-month contract with options at $150 weekly. Norma and her mother promptly packed and left for Hollywood. Her introduction to Mayer

NORMA SHEARER

also brought Norma into contact with Irving Thalberg, boy genius of the Metro studio, who would play a decidedly important role both in her personal and private life.

Norma was immediately cast in *The Wanters,* and on the basis of her screen test director John Stahl demoted her from the lead to a bit role. Placed under the direction of Reginald Barker in her next film, *Pleasure Mad,* Norma was nervous and clashed with Barker several times before Mayer called her into his office. In his infamous fatherly manner, he told her to shape up or forget her option. Thalberg arrived with the good news (for Norma) that the scenes already taken were so photographically bad that they would all have to be retaken. Given this reprieve, Norma's determination to succeed won out over her inability to get along with Barker and Mayer was satisfied with her performance.

This passion for success was a grim determination on an order similar to that possessed by Gloria Swanson, but Miss Shearer started with much less experience (and some would say little talent) which put her at a handicap. Yet Norma quickly became a popular loan-

Miss Shearer on location. Notice the violin in left foreground for mood music.

out actress, and in her first year on Mayer's payroll she appeared in eight pictures. Each showed a definite improvement over her previous performances, and before long she was doing fairly well in the lesser films which the studio released. *He Who Gets Slapped* was her biggest break and working with Lon Chaney boosted her confidence. Nice little programmers like *The Snob, The Lady of the Night* and *The Devil's Circus* followed, and by 1927 Norma had reached a secondary level of stardom, well below that of Pickford, Gish and Swanson, but comfortably above her status of just a few years before.

1927 marked a definite turn for the better in her career; she had been dating Irving Thalberg casually when he suddenly proposed. She accepted and they were married that September. From this point on, her roles were carefully chosen; the director for the picture was hand-picked and everything was done to properly package Norma for audience reception. This was no reflection on Norma or her talent—Thalberg had an uncanny knack for intuitively feeling what was right and wrong in the making of a picture and he also possessed that rarest of qualities in the Hollywood of the twenties—honesty. Her husband had great confidence in Norma's talent and believed sincerely that if she were properly presented on the screen

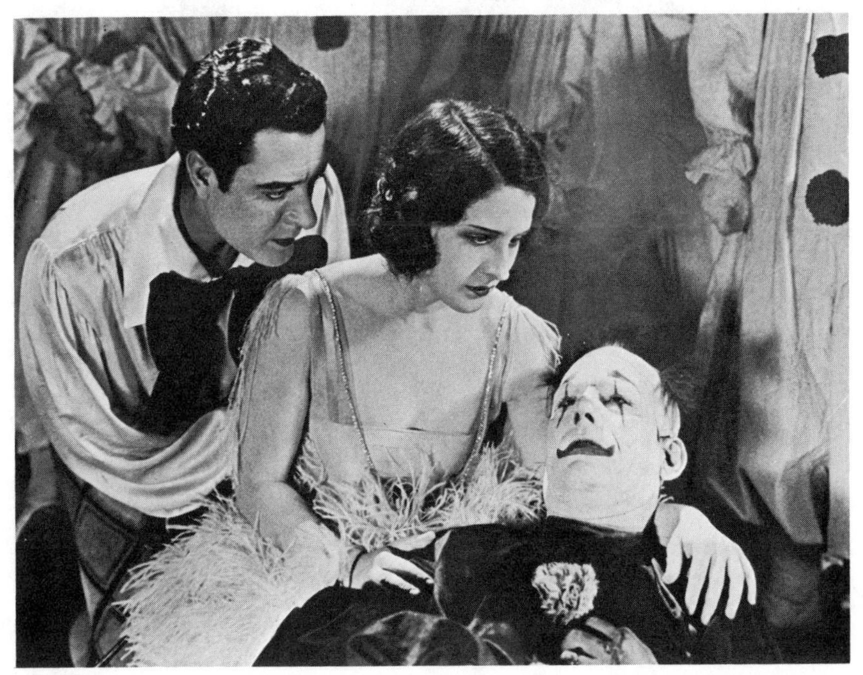

John Gilbert, Norma, and Lon Chaney in *He Who Gets Slapped.*

Norma and her husband, Irving Thalberg, in the early thirties.

in the right stories, she would more than justify the production money backing her career.

Far from being a great actress, Norma did manage to get by with a style somewhere between genuine acting and pantomime. Her best roles were those requiring deep emotion, and while she handled everything with an extensive repertoire of expression

The Actress.

***The Student Prince,* with Jean Hersholt and Ramon Novarro.**

Norma and John Miljan in *The Devil's Circus.*

changes, a passing moment of emotion was a challenge to which she could rise. However the deep, raging emotional fires of a *Madame X* were beyond her capabilities and Thalberg wisely steered her away from such roles. By the time sound arrived, Norma's career was on a sure footing, and with her husband at the helm she had no fear that the talkies would torpedo her career.

Lon Chaney, Norma, and Claire MacDowell in *Tower of Lies.*

Appearing in M-G-M's first all-talking drama, *The Trial of Mary Dugan* (taken from a then-popular Broadway courtroom play), Norma went on to star in several of the studio's choice roles like *Strange Interlude* and *Idiot's Delight,* and until Thalberg's untimely death in September 1936, she was a money-making property for Mayer and company. But with his demise, Norma announced her retirement from the screen. A rather complicated settlement of her contract and her husband's share in M-G-M led to her commitment to do six more pictures. At this point, her carefully plotted career began to falter and come apart at the seams. She did not get the right stories and the directors who could have best handled her were always busy on some other property. Unwisely turning down the leads in both *Gone With the Wind* and *Mrs. Miniver,* she decided that she should do light comedy instead and after a few rather shallow pictures (*The Women, We Were Dancing, The Cardboard Lover*), she left the screen in 1942 to marry Martin Arrougé, a Sun Valley ski instructor. Unlike many other stars who "retired," Norma has not shown any interest in returning to the screen, but

With Conrad Nagel in *Excuse Me.*

is presently working on her autobiography, which should make interesting reading for those who remember the golden era in which she rose to stardom.

GLORIA SWANSON

Beyond a doubt the most regal queen the silent screen ever knew, Gloria Swanson went out of her way to make certain that everyone was aware of it; Mary Pickford, Lillian Gish and Greta Garbo were screen stars but La Swanson was THE star of stars. When Gloria took a trip abroad, the press covered the event as if royalty were involved and her long-standing personal (and public) feud with Pola Negri in the mid-twenties, which ostensibly began over the studio cats but was really a war for the studio supremacy which Gloria held, kept gossip columnists busy and Gloria's name constantly before the public. She also indulged in the "royalty-for-a-mate" game popular among the Hollywood heroines, snaring one with the impressive name of Marquis Henri de la Falaise de Coudray for her third husband; only the biggest and best was good enough for Gloria. And it all came about in such an unlikely manner.

The daughter of an Army officer, Gloria first appeared at the old Chicago Essanay studio and is said to have been briefly considered by Chaplin along with Edna Purviance as a possible leading lady but rejected as being too "cold"—a statement roundly denied by both principals. Having married an ex-elephant trainer and comedian named Wallace Beery, who was tiring of his female impersonation in the "Sweedie" series, Gloria's stay at Essanay was brief, as Beery wanted to work for Keystone.

Keystone business manager George W. Stout and Mack Sennett agreed to hire Beery, but the comic also persuaded them to hire his wife sight unseen, thus doubling his family income. Once on the lot, few directors found much work for Beery, who spent most of his

GLORIA SWANSON

time doing nothing. But Sennett teamed Gloria with little Bobby Vernon in a series of light romantic comedies which struck a responsive chord with the public, who enjoyed her striking appearance and deadpan approach to humor. Gloria proved to be a considerable departure from the run-of-the-mill comic heroine which Sennett's comedies customarily featured. During this time, life with Wally Beery was not peaches and cream, but Gloria took her lot staunchly, showing up at the studio much earlier than necessary on many occasions to perfect her make-up and cover the bruises meted

Gloria and Bobby Vernon, 1916.

***Male and Female*, 1919.**

out by a husband whose professional jealousy and pride had been deflated by her success and his apparent failure. This routine continued until Gloria felt her career to be on firm ground, then she and Beery parted company.

When Sennett took his leave of Triangle in 1917, Gloria was one of the few chosen to accompany The King of Comedy; Bobby Vernon's contract remained with Triangle. By this time, Gloria had decided that slapstick comedy, bathing suits and pratfalls were not the roads she wished to take toward stardom and left the Sennett lot, returning to Triangle where she quickly acquired the lead in *You Can't Believe Everything*. From there, it was just a hop, skip and jump through several Triangle films to the waiting set of Cecil B. deMille, who was about to write a new chapter in cinema history with his slick bedroom farces like *Don't Change Your Husband, Why Change Your Wife?, For Better or Worse* and *Male and Female*. These deMille comedies were light, frothy and tantalizingly suggestive for their day, giving Gloria some of the best publicized and exploited bathing scenes ever put on celluloid. When Gloria Swanson left deMille and Paramount to strike out on her own, she turned to emotional tear-jerkers and soon had the box-office wrapped around her little finger. Returning from Europe after filming *Madame Sans Gene* in 1925, Gloria reacted to Adolph Zukor's offer of $18,000 weekly with a flat NO—she wished to make her own pictures and whatever Gloria wanted, Gloria did. It's hard to imagine very many stars turning down that kind of cash, even if the contract *was* only for forty weeks a year, but money meant little to a *real* star and the once-timid Gloria Swanson had traveled a long road from the days when Wallace Beery drank and gambled away her paycheck a week before she earned it.

Driving ambition was probably Gloria's most striking attribute beyond her strange, unusual beauty. Although her films lacked importance beyond the box-office and her career, they were well-made and exploitable attractions which gave Gloria the opportunity to act her head off. The ambition to become a someone, a celebrity and a star led Gloria to throw everything she had into each role. Her flamboyant performances, often ranging from tenderness to the

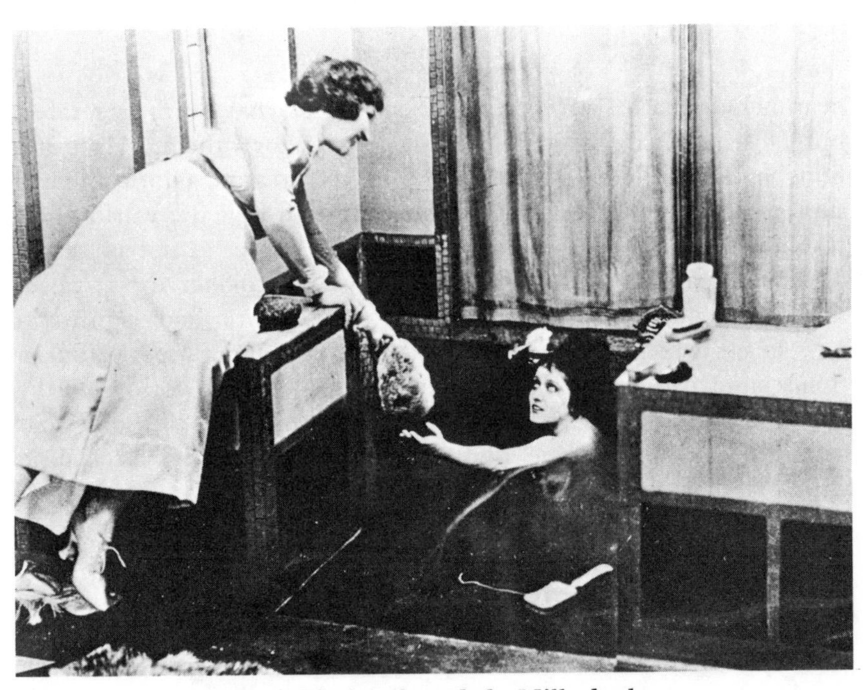

One of Gloria's famed de Mille baths.

***Under the Lash,* 1921.**

near-melodramatic, were theatrical and somewhat overexaggerated, but fans loved her in spite of (or perhaps for) them. While her films appear a bit dated today for this very reason, Gloria reigned supreme in the twenties and she made certain that the world knew it. Showmanship was as much a part of her career as it was for deMille, the past master of the art who had taught her the value of the right kind of publicity. Over the years, Gloria had acquired a new image which fairly oozed good breeding and proper enunciation, commensurate with her stature in the celluloid world, and the Gloria Swanson of 1925 was a world removed from the somewhat awkward Chicago gamine who had despised her brief association with Mack Sennett a decade before.

While the Swanson career continued into the sound era with ease (Gloria's voice proved quite satisfactory), she made only a handful of films before retiring. Many years later, she would come out of retirement to triumphantly cap her career with a magnificent portrayal as the faded movie queen Norma Desmond in *Sunset Boulevard* (1950), earning plaudits from those very critics who had

Her Husband's Trademark, **1922.**

steadfastly maintained through the years that she really could not act at all.

Pola Negri had tried, but only Joan Crawford at the height of her career ever came close to challenging glamorous, glorious Gloria

With Valentino in *Beyond the Rocks,* 1922.

The Love of Sunya, 1927.

***Sadie Thompson,* 1928. Raoul Walsh (l) directed and played the male lead.**

for the title of Movie Queen. Symbolic of the movies' golden age, Gloria has long been a part of the folklore surrounding the screen and her Norma Desmond, which brought forth a scornful "None of us floozies were *that* nuts!" from Mae Murray was no more improbable than La Swanson herself. Unlike many of her contemporaries, Gloria Swanson lives for the present and is very reluctant to reminisce about the old days. Indeed, she is a frequent guest on TV talk shows, where she states without hesitation her own strong opinions on the problems and issues of today. But should she ever choose to join the growing list of ex-stars now marketing their memoirs in book form, it should make delightful reading.

BLANCHE SWEET

The incurably romantic nature of D. W. Griffith led him to invariably feature a particular type of heroine in his picture. His attraction to delicate, slim-bodied young girls with a winsome frailty was perhaps best exemplified by Lillian Gish, and to a lesser extent, Mary Pickford and Mae Marsh. Blanche Sweet managed to join these three as one of Griffith's favorite heroines by talent alone; she certainly did not live up to the director's ideal of womanhood. Blanche was neither slim of body nor did she exude frailty; there was a hardy air of determination about her that lent itself nicely to roles in which the heroine had to fend for herself and Miss Sweet (her real name) certainly projected the ability to take care of herself with little or no help from whatever male support happened to be cast with her.

Like Pickford, Blanche was already a veteran of the stage when she joined Biograph early in Griffith's reign. Born in Chicago, tutored by her grandmother and educated in California, she had first appeared on the stage at the tender age of 3½, eventually appearing with stars like Chauncey Olcott before trying her luck in the movies during a slump in theatrical engagements. Miss Sweet soon became one of Griffith's regularly featured heroines and although her screen career lasted until early in the thirties, she is still best remembered for her strong-willed portrayals in Griffith films like *The Battle,* a significant and definite predecessor to *The Birth of a Nation; The Lonedale Operator,* one of the most famous of Griffith's early innovative efforts; *The Avenging Conscience,* a psychological drama heavily indebted to Poe and *Judith of Bethulia,* acknowledged as the first American "spectacle" film.

BLANCHE SWEET

With Henry B. Walthall in *Judith of Bethulia,* 1914.

The Lonedale Operator remains a fascinating exercise in the early use of dramatic cross-cutting as the telegrapher (Blanche) held off bandits while awaiting the arrival of help. This short film was almost certainly the culmination of a technique Griffith had been developing for quite some time and gave Blanche an opportunity at both romantic comedy and tense melodrama. *The Avenging Conscience* is not so impressive a film today as when released over a half-century ago; it remains interesting mainly because of the fascinating touch of ambiguity with which Miss Sweet embellished her portrayal of Annabel. But it was in *Judith of Bethulia,* Griffith's final Biograph, that Blanche could be said to have completely "arrived." Cast as the Jewish widow who by deception gains entrance into the camp of the Assyrian Holofernes, and decapitates the enemy general in spite of having fallen in love with him, it was the type of role no other Griffith heroine could have handled so well and Blanche scored heavily.

One of the earliest of the Griffith heroines to leave the fold, Blanche moved to Jesse Lasky's lot in 1915 where she was quickly starred in a lengthy series of strong and varied dramas, including *The Warrens of Virginia, Stolen Goods* and *The Secret Sin*. She also found out just how much the years with Griffith had restricted her development as an actress. Working under D. W. did not necessarily guarantee a well-rounded screen personality and the Lasky series called upon her for a great variety of portrayals. It proved a profitable training ground and one which expanded her versatility.

The Case of Becky required Blanche to enact a dual personality; *The Blacklist* demanded a strong melodramatic approach and *The Ragamuffin* carried an artistic touch in Blanche's role as a girl rescued from a life of thievery. By the time she left the Lasky lot, Blanche Sweet was an accomplished actress, but one whose career in the twenties failed to really attract the public's attention. Married in 1922 to director Marshall Neilan, Blanche worked with her husband in many of her pictures during the twenties. A versatile talent behind the megaphone, Neilan was sufficiently capable to rise to a dramatic challenge, but the assignments handed him too seldom placed such demands on his abilities, especially at M-G-M. In a sense, Blanche Sweet's career suffered from the same malaise

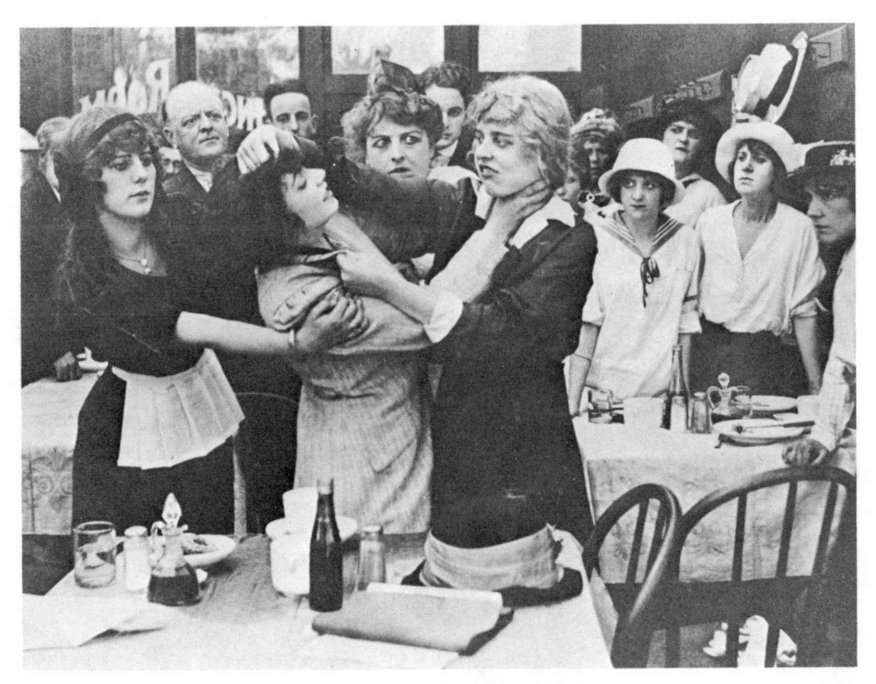

***The Case of Becky*, 1915.**

Stolen Goods, 1915.

The Blacklist, 1916.

With Tommy Meighan in *The Silent Partner,* 1917.

In the Palace of the King, 1923.

Anna Christie, 1923.

With Ronald Colman in *His Supreme Moment*, 1925.

Blanche learns the secret of *The Woman in White,* 1929.

that affected Alice Terry's (whom she somewhat resembled in appearance), but Neilan did not have the financial backing to step outside the system as Rex Ingram had. In spite of her poignant performances in *Tess of the D'Urbervilles* and the first screen version of *Anna Christie,* Blanche just never seemed able to escape identification with Griffith and the early days.

Her marriage to Neilan ended in divorce in 1929, and after completing her third talkie, *The Silver Horde* (RKO), Blanche left Hollywood in 1931 for the New York stage. Marrying Ray Hackett in 1936, she virtually dropped out of sight until 1958, when television producer Edgar Peterson found her clerking in a New York City department store. He brought Blanche back for a new generation in *The Secret Love of Johnny Spain,* but the "comeback" was a brief one and Blanche Sweet lives quietly today in New York, still remembered best for her part in those formative years on the screen.

NORMA TALMADGE

There were as many paths to stardom on the silent screen as there were actresses seeking that golden fleece. Some of its heroines brought so much talent and popularity with them that their bid for fame could not have failed; others reached the same goal by sheer perseverance and hard work, and in between these two extremes lay several hundred combinations for success.

Sometimes it seemed that lady luck played a major role. All the evidence appears to favor this interpretation in the case of Norma Talmadge. When Vitagraph had decided that she was really not an actress after all (and therefore a luxury on the player roster), her career was saved by the intervention of actor Maurice Costello, whose influence with Albert E. Smith turned the tide. A few years later, Norma's career was going nowhere in particular when she married Joseph Schenck, a former booking manager for the Loews theater chain. Schenck had recently left his position to produce independently for Lewis J. Selznick and once he and Norma were wed, Loews suddenly began booking and exploiting her films, giving Norma Talmadge an exposure her career had lacked. Schenck continued to remain a production power in the industry throughout the twenties and Norma, cast in well-produced and carefully chosen pictures, became a household name.

Historians and critics still have not resolved the matter of Norma's histrionic abilities; Paul Rotha and Iris Barry have both gone on record supporting the opinion that she could not act at all; Edward Wagenknecht countered this view with his opinion that she never gave a poor performance and Joe Franklin compared Norma as roughly equivalent in her time to Greer Garson. Person-

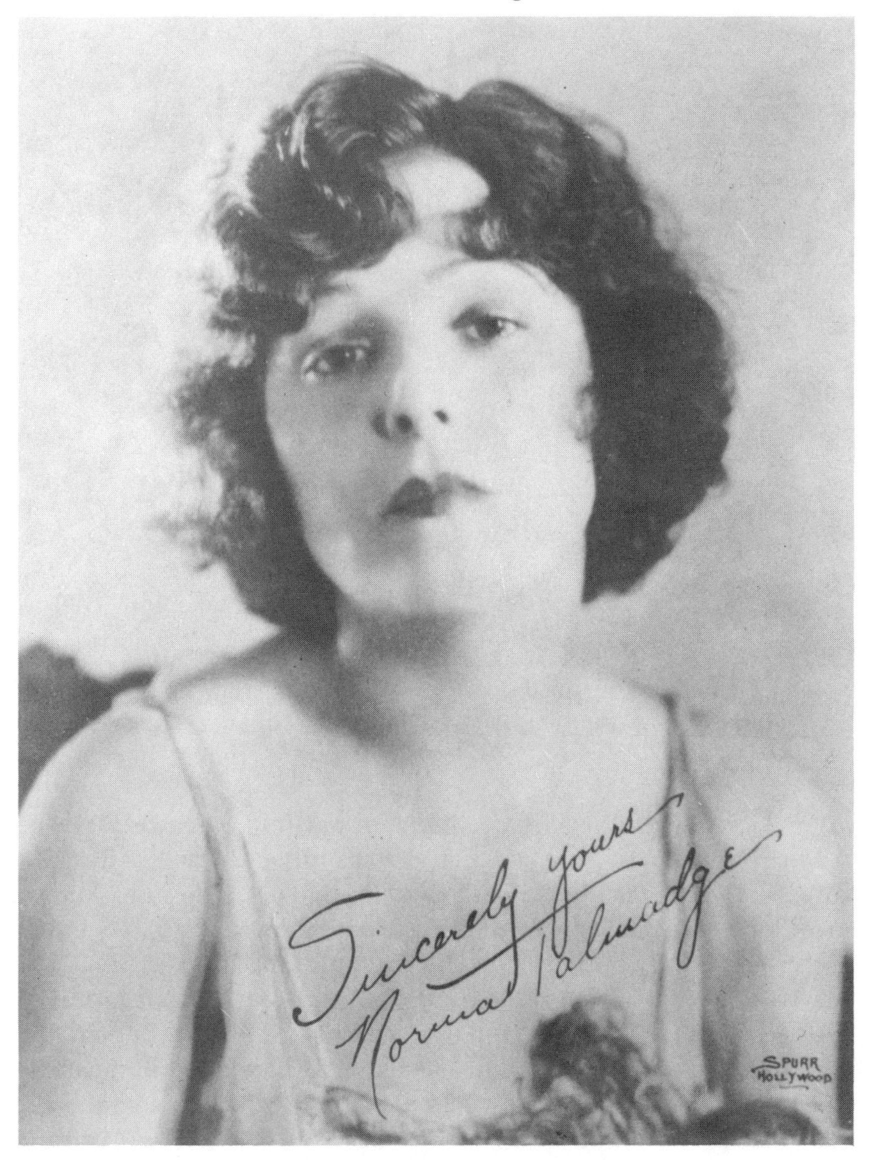

NORMA TALMADGE

ally, I find Norma a charming light comedienne but never having developed a liking or much of a tolerance for the soap operas in which she found her real fame after World War I, I have often found it difficult to sit through some of her films.

A Brooklyn girl who set her sights on screen stardom early in life (both hers and the screen's), Norma started at Vitagraph

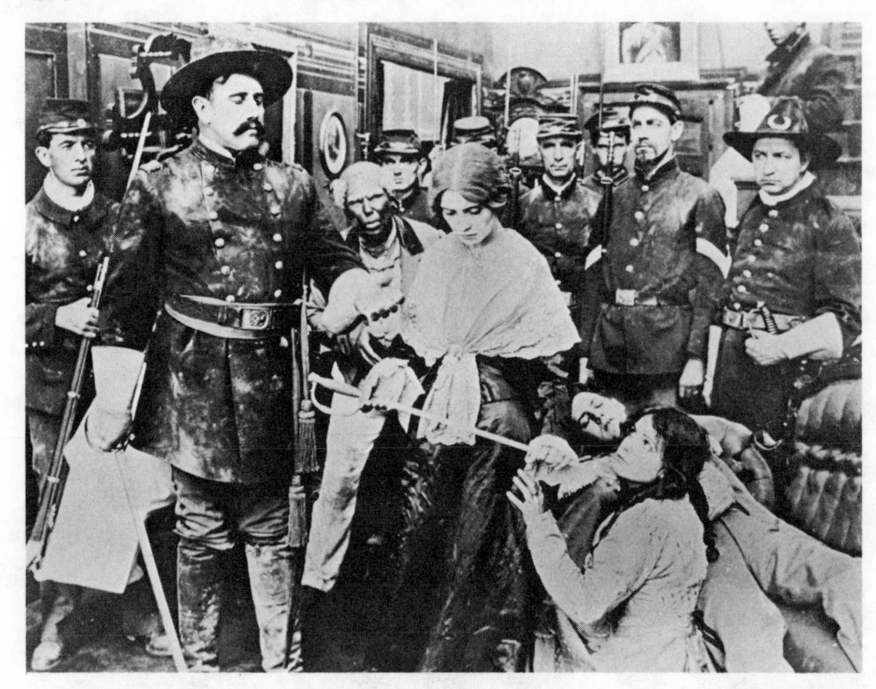

Norma kneeling at Carlyle Blackwell's feet in *A Dixie Mother,* 1910. Florence Turner (center) hands his saber to William Shea.

around 1910 where her first really important role was with Florence Turner in *A Dixie Mother,* often erroneously cited as her first picture. *A Tale of Two Cities* with Costello remains as her best-known work for Vitagraph, and when she joined Triangle in 1916 Norma's career was hardly outstanding—she had appeared in many films but few had left any lasting impression. An attractive but not beautiful girl, her stay at Triangle did not exactly set the world on fire. Almost from its very beginnings, Triangle had been in financial difficulties and its poorly exploited pictures with expensive stage stars had failed miserably at the box-office.[1] In an effort to turn the tide, low-budget productions using players easily recognized by audiences were tried and Norma was cast in a series of interesting but insignificant comic-dramas like *The Social Secretary.*

But it was during her Triangle days that Joe Schenck needed a star and began pressing his case. His contact with Norma brought

1. Mr. Lahue tells the tragicomic story of the rise and fall of the Triangle Film Corporation in *Dreams for Sale* (South Brunswick and New York: A.S. Barnes and Company, 1971).

As an ambitious young girl in *The Social Secretary,* 1916.

Schenck both an actress and a wife, and the Norma Talmadge Film Corporation was established in late 1916. Films like *Panthea, Poppy* and *The Forbidden City* gave Norma a chance to display her full capabilities for the first time, and with the forceful Schenck behind the helm, the Talmadge career swung into high gear.

Norma's most active and popular period came in the early twenties with pictures like *The Sign on the Door, The Branded Woman, Passion Flower* and *Within the Law,* melodramatic tear

Norma and Seena Owen in *Martha's Vindication,* 1916.

jerkers which allowed her to suffer long and nobly. Once Schenck caught on to his wife's popularity as the heroine who fought for love against tragic and overwhelming odds but eventually won, the die was cast and Norma spent the twenties suffering on-screen in

Norma found it necessary to employ a disguise to keep men away.

***The Voice From the Minaret,* 1923.**

***Camille*, 1927.**

every conceivable situation that first-class writers like Mary Murillo, Anita Loos and Frances Marion could devise. Schenck had now widened the scope of his activities, featuring Norma's sister Constance in a series of farce comedies like *Lessons in Love, Wedding*

***Du Barry, Woman of Passion,* 1930.**

Bells and *Dulcy,* which also won at the box-office. Laughter or tears, he could provide both to theater patrons.

The Schenck productions were top-notch and the money spent on each was used to surround Norma with just the right amount of lavish atmosphere. Talented directors like Frank Lloyd, Herbert Brenon and Fred Niblo translated the scripts to the screen and Norma's stature as an actress was considerable by the latter twenties, when she appeared in a modernized version of *Camille.* At this time, she moved her releasing company from First National to United Artists. Although Schenck continued to manage her business affairs, the two had separated in 1926.

Norma made but two appearances in talkies and when critics panned her *Du Barry,* Norma decided to quit while she was at the top. She had watched her salary grow from $25 a week to $250,000 yearly, and between her mother's insistence that the daughters establish a trust fund and Schenck's careful management of their financial affairs, both Norma and Constance (who had also retired with the coming of sound) were no longer dependent upon their careers. Norma passed the thirties with a marriage to George Jessel and her own radio show; the forties found her enjoying a third marriage to Dr. Carvel James.

While her name never quite had the same ring of stardom that a Lillian Gish, Gloria Swanson or Mary Pickford evoked, Norma's fans were legion in spite of the fact that very few of her more than 250 pictures could be called important. Norma Talmadge and Lady Luck enjoyed a lengthy and profitable relationship which ended Dec. 24, 1957 when she died from pneumonia. A wave of nostalgia tempered the Christmas spirit of many who remembered those bitter-sweet hours spent in the local movie palaces many years before, softly weeping as their favorite heroine silently suffered one calamity after another in her search for true love. Times have changed considerably since Norma was at the top; we have become a very impersonal nation whose emotional responses are often tinged with hypocrisy, and no heroine could ever suffer her way to stardom these days as did Norma Talmadge, but doesn't it all make you wonder . . . and long just a bit for the old days?

ALICE TERRY

The brief screen career of lovely Alice Terry is inseparably entwined with the story of director Rex Ingram's rise and fall. While Alice worked with such stellar male attractions as Rudolph Valentino and Ramon Novarro in the twenties, she appeared mainly in her husband's productions. As a consequence, she endured long periods of self-imposed exile from the screen and out of public view. The 17-year-old Miss Terry had fallen in love with the director in 1920 when her first real break came in the form of a role in Ingram's *Hearts Are Trumps.* Not only did little Alice Taaffe from Vincennes, Indiana, get along famously with the handsome Ingram in private life; he was the first to recognize a spark of talent in the struggling young actress, whose career as an extra and bit player dated back to Triangle days.

When *The Four Horsemen of the Apocalypse* established Valentino as an overnight box-office sensation, Ingram's smash hit of 1921 allowed the director and Miss Terry to practically write their own ticket at Metro. This financial and artistic blockbuster was followed by pictures like *The Conquering Power, The Prisoner of Zenda* and *Scaramouche,* a group not quite as profitable but equally well received critically. With such a string of successful screen epics behind them, the Ingrams became Metro's uncrowned royalty, and late in 1923 left for North Africa where Miss Terry and Novarro cavorted in the sand in Metro's contribution to the "Sheik" craze, *The Arab.*

From a rather mousy looking supporting actress at Triangle in 1918, Alice Terry had turned into the glamorous picture of self-confidence in her leading roles, a tribute both to Ingram's sure

ALICE TERRY

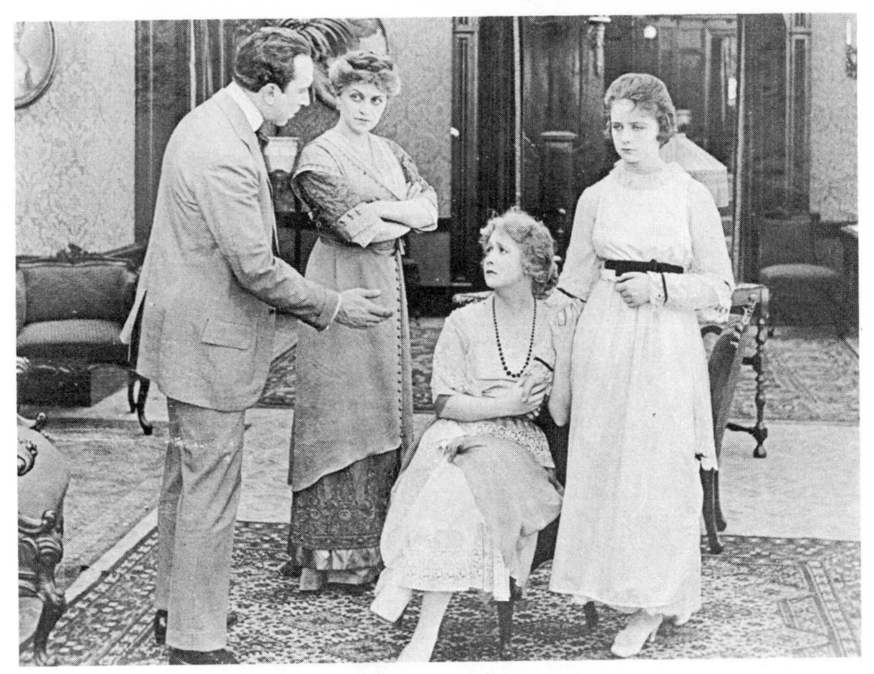

With Bessie Barriscale in *Not My Sister,* 1916.

hand and loving care. Although a very good actress in the roles she played for Ingram, Alice had little opportunity to display versatility as a performer, endowing her heroines with either a winsome, unaffected appeal (as in *The Conquering Power*) or the stately serenity of bejeweled loveliness necessary for Ruritanian romance (like *The Prisoner of Zenda*). Heavy, fiery melodramatics did not seem to be her metier but Alice made a perfect heroine for the pictorial beauty and exotic atmosphere with which Ingram embued his stylistic screen interpretations. Her fame might easily have been much greater, but her films usually featured a male star who caught the public's fancy and her fine work was overlooked as a result. Fortunately for Miss Terry, she was content to bask in the reflection of her husband's glory.

When they returned from Africa in early 1924, Ingram found Metro ready to announce its consolidation with Goldwyn. Unhappy with the prospect, the director sought counsel from Marcus Loew and Nick Schenck, who agreed to finance his films, and so the Ingrams moved back to Europe, settling near Nice, France. There he produced *Mare Nostrum, The Magician* and *The Garden of Allah,*

Alice's fine performance as Marguerite Laurier in *The Four Horsemen of the Apocalypse* (1921) was overshadowed by public acclaim for the unknown Rudolph Valentino as Julio.

all starring his lovely wife. The films were critically acclaimed, but none was as financially satisfying as his previous efforts.

The coming of sound destroyed Ingram, whose obsession with pictorial form, atmosphere, lighting and mood did not blend well with the new medium. Neither he nor Alice Terry made any further films and little was heard from them over the years, save for an occasional visit back to the United States. In the early fifties a rather tasteless version of Valentino's life appeared on the screen starring mirror-image Anthony Dexter as the Latin Lover. *Valentino* hinted openly at a love affair between Rudy and his first leading lady, and while the names had been changed, Miss Terry, who recognized a highly uncomplimentary slur against her character when she saw it, sued the studio for misrepresentation, and won an out of court settlement.

Rex Ingram died July 21, 1950, but Alice Terry remains a

***The Conquering Power,* 1921.**

North Hollywood resident who prefers to stay out of the limelight. Her career ended over forty years ago, and she does not continually dredge up old memories, trading on the past as have some of her contemporaries in recent years. Miss Terry was one of the few

With Lewis Stone and Stuart Holmes in *The Prisoner of Zenda,* 1922.

A sultry portrait of Alice while filming *Mare Nostrum* in 1926. Ten years had made a great difference in the meek-looking little girl who appeared in Triangle Plays.

With the famous French clown Grock at the Ingram studio in Nice during the filming of *The Garden of Allah,* 1927.

actresses who should have made more films and expanded her acting range, for she was always a treat to behold on the screen and her gracious beauty often made me regret that I was not born a decade or two earlier.

FLORENCE VIDOR

Although she never rose to top stardom on the screen, the dependable and versatile Florence Vidor was certainly one of the busiest and most accomplished heroines of the silent drama during the twenties. Leaving their native Texas, Florence and her husband, King Vidor, set out to earn their living in motion pictures. They both did quite well for themselves; King Vidor became one of the decade's most respected directors while Florence began her own career at Vitagraph with small roles after paying a visit to her friend Corrine Griffith. By 1917, she had moved into high gear with a role opposite William Farnum in Fox's *A Tale of Two Cities.*

The lady worked for just about every producing company in the twenties, appearing in such diverse vehicles as *The Virginian* with Kenneth Harlan, deMille's *Old Wives for New,* Lubitsch's *The Patriot,* Frank Lloyd's *Eagle of the Sea* and Tom Ince's *Lying Lips, Christine of the Hungry Heart* and *Barbara Frietchie.* Readers familiar with these pictures will recognize the wide range of parts in which Miss Vidor played, but she was most at ease with comedy and became quite popular in a sparkling lightweight series after signing with Paramount in 1925. Her roles in *Are Parents People?* and *The Grand Duchess and the Waiter* with Adolphe Menjou surely remain among her best performances. Whether in rags or period costumes, Florence was absolutely lovely and producers knew that she could deliver with a consistency that few of their other secondary stars possessed.

There were two opposing schools of acting prevalent on the

FLORENCE VIDOR

***Old Wives For New,* 1918.**

silent screen, a kind of flamboyant overacting left over from the stage and a natural, realistic style developed by the picture people. Like all competent actresses at the time, Florence Vidor was equally adept in either; her role in *The Virginian* was nicely handled without overly melodramatic emphasis, while in *Eagle of the Sea* she

Florence and Jack Holt in *The Honor of His House,* 1918.

With House Peters in *Lying Lips,* 1921.

***Main Street*, with Monte Blue and Alan Hale, 1923.**

***Christine of the Hungry Heart* with ~~Ian Keith~~, 1924.**

Clive Brook

Lew Cody, Lewis Stone and Florence in *Husbands and Lovers,* 1924.

appeared as reactive as a 1916 serial heroine constantly in danger. Whatever the director wished, he could be certain that Miss Vidor would put it across effectively and with just the right touches he demanded. This ability to deliver to order accounted for a large measure of her success during a very busy and profitable decade for Florence.

But separate careers and the success that accompanied each broke up her marriage; the Vidors had separated in 1923 and were divorced later. In August 1928, reporters heard rumors of a quiet wedding ceremony performed by a Supreme Court justice at his hotel and discovered that the bride and bridegroom involved were no less than Florence and Jascha Heifetz, a young violinist just beginning his rise to musical prominence. Florence gave up her career and became simply Mrs. Heifetz, traveling with her husband on tours and bearing him two children. Their divorce in the forties came as a great surprise to neighbors who had viewed their marriage as ideal.

Looking back today on a career that was one of the foundations of the silent screen drama, Florence has few if any regrets and is

With Betty Bronson and Adolphe Menjou in *Are Parents People?*, 1925.

Tempted by Emil Jannings in *The Patriot*, 1928.

seriously thinking of writing her autobiography. If and when she does, it should make fascinating reading, for Miss Vidor's career crossed that of virtually every important producer and director in the business and she should have some very fascinating comments on the formative years of the cinema.

FANNIE WARD

When Fannie Ward died in January 1952, hers was a name which meant nothing to those of us in our teens and early twenties; but to Dad and Grandfather, Fannie's death brought back many fond memories of "The Eternal Flapper." While Miss Ward was better known to the public for an amazing ability to retain her youthful appearance, she was one of Paramount's leading female heroines in the 1913–19 period. Although somewhere in the neighborhood of 40 to 45 years old at that time, she did not look a day over 24 in her films. Fannie's age and birthdate were topics close to her heart and whenever either were mentioned, she merely laughed off the question with some ridiculous reply. When she died of a cerebral hemorrhage, obituaries speculated that she was in her seventies or eighties; no one really knew for certain.

Born Fannie Ward Buchanan, her early predisposition toward the stage eventually cost her the love and respect of her father. He disowned his daughter when she and her mother traveled East to meet with Daniel Frohman, the famed theatrical producer. Fannie had won a local beauty and talent contest and this solidified her ambition; mother seconded the girl's desires and abetted her entry into show business. Very much impressed with the young girl, Frohman suggested that she drop the Buchanan, then helped her get the part of Cupid in the Broadway play *Pippino,* which opened in 1890. Over the next two decades, Miss Ward acquired a solid reputation for her theatrical interpretations, and in 1913 she moved into pictures with Jesse L. Lasky's Feature Film Company. After spending nearly two years in minor roles, interspersed with stage work, she was given the leading female role in "The

FANNIE WARD

***The Gutter Magdalene,* 1916.**

Cheat" and playing opposite Sessue Hayakawa, Fannie turned in an excellent performance. The film was an immediate smash hit with critics and fans alike, establishing both performers as stars. Miss Ward spent several more years headlining the release schedule for Paramount before returning to the stage. Her films were extremely well-received by women, who seemed to be highly attracted to Fannie's work. This is not to say that she had few male admirers; after all, a good looking girl like Fannie could turn heads wherever she went.

Fannie had already turned the heads of royalty in Europe, setting both London and Paris in an uproar by her marriage in 1900 to the prominent London financier Joseph Lewis. He promptly bedecked his wife in what was reputed to be $1 million worth of jewels and began calling upon his titled friends. Although well-received (at least on the surface) by her husband's acquaintances, it was his male friends who were most receptive to her charms. Thus Miss Ward was an international celebrity several years before entering the exalted realm of motion picture stars. The marriage did not last, however, and Fannie eventually married her former leading man, Jack Dean.

Her screen roles were many and varied. They were always well-written and produced to give her the opportunity to show off her fabulous figure and face. While she often toyed with semi-comic roles somewhat in the Mary Pickford vein, she was at her best in deep drama and stark tragedy. To place this kind of role in the setting of an elaborate costume or historical play was even more to her liking, for this gave Fannie a chance to wear gorgeous clothes and make-up, changing both often in each film. There just may have been more than a touch of envy which attracted her female fans to Fannie's pictures. Reviewers often commented that it was her personal charm and magnetism which carried the pictures off, pointing out that while she was given good support by the others in the cast, the films were usually Fannie's alone. Unfortunately, it's almost impossible to pass judgment on her work today, as few of Fannie's pictures have been seen for decades. In all likelihood, the majority of her screen work has disappeared from view forever.

Fanny and Jack Dean in *Betty to the Rescue,* 1917.

Fannie's love of costumes and make-up was reflected in scripts like *The Winning of Sally Temple,* 1917.

Leaving pictures in the early twenties, Fannie went back to Broadway and the stage, where she continued to play young heroines until well into the thirties. She finally retired after her daughter's tragic death in an airplane crash in 1938. In spite of her age (or

***Each Pearl a Tear,* 1916.**

Tense drama was Fannie's real forte.

Fannie Ward in *The Cheat*, a C. B. de Mille production.

because of it), Fannie retained a strong fascination for the stylish clothes of the younger generation and columnists dubbed her "Sparkling Fannie"—her fabled jewels continued to adorn the neckline of the current season's fashions.

All this time, life seemed to be passing everyone by except Fannie and she continued to appear youthful and attractive well into her fifties and sixties. Cautious and coy about references to her appearance, Miss Ward was forever dreaming up some new answer to the question of how she stayed so young. At first, she relied upon the rather mundane explanation that it was due to the fact she had always enjoyed a carefully regulated diet which kept her weight exactly at 100 pounds. Then she added facial exercises as a sop to the millions of admiring women who would have given anything for her secret. Next, she speculated that it was the power of positive thinking; always keeping her mind in tune with the times and never letting her mental capabilities fall into the rut of worry. Fannie's final admission on the subject attributed the miracle to facial creams and their application, the content of which were a secret taught her by the famed French stage star, Gaby Deslys (who had also retained an amazingly youthful appearance through most of her career).

The mere suggestion that she had undergone plastic surgery was enough to throw Fannie into near uncontrollable rage and she once offered a huge sum of money to anyone who could prove that she had ever had her face "lifted". While no one ever did decipher exactly what had kept Fannie young in appearance far beyond her age, there was no doubting that she had something the average woman lacked and whatever that something was went to the grave with her. Beyond the mention of facial creams, Fannie would say nothing more on the subject. Her personal stationery was engraved with the two words, ETERNAL YOUTH, and while Fannie led an active, strenuous life as the toast of two continents for over four decades, she firmly believed that accomplishing her motto was possible. But death took her husband Jack Dean in 1950 and a good deal of Fannie's zest for living died with him. Two years later, she passed away. The heroine of an intriguing play more interesting than any of her stage or screen roles was gone.

KATHLYN WILLIAMS

Down through the years, some screen heroines have become strongly identified with a particular role or film and usually it is one that is not even representative of their abilities or career. For example, mention Pearl White today and the association which immediately springs to mind is the primitive *The Perils of Pauline;* Pauline Frederick stands out as *Madame X* and Kathlyn Williams is remembered for her performance in *The Adventures of Kathlyn,* Selig's 1913 chapter play which started a serial craze that did not abate until 1956.

A Butte, Montana, girl, the regal Miss Williams was 22 when she entered pictures with Biograph in 1910. Her stage career started with touring stock companies and eventually brought her to the Sargent Dramatic School and Broadway. *All Is Not Gold* gave Kathlyn her first screen role, but she remained with Biograph only a short time, appearing the same year at Selig's Chicago studio. In no time at all, Kathlyn was in great demand, playing every conceivable role from ingenue to little old lady, and in the process avoiding any possibility of type casting. But in spite of her best efforts, Kathlyn's Selig films identified her with wild animal pictures. (Selig's prime asset was a collection of highly trained animals, and in many of his pictures the human actors were secondary in importance to his performing zoo.) Holding much the same fascination for fans as the circus, Selig's release schedule contained a high percentage of jungle and animal pictures and Kathlyn became especially effective at portraying fright, uttering the silent shriek of terror as four-footed danger appeared.

KATHLYN WILLIAMS, The Selig Girl.

While she balanced her career with appearances in other dramatic films and several of the early Tom Mix westerns (the best of which was *Chip of the Flying U*), it was *The Adventures of Kathlyn* that elevated the Selig Girl to her pedestal in the early hall of stardom. Couples danced to a hesitation waltz named in her honor, sipping Kathlyn cocktails between sets; the ladies wore

Kathlyn with Charles West, Guy Oliver, and Eugenie Besserer in an early Selig drama.

Kathlyn as "The Unwilling Queen" in *The Adventures of Kathlyn,* Selig's 1913 serial which assured her of undying cinema fame.

With Roy Stewart in *The U. P. Trail*, 1920.

Kathlyn often portrayed the errant society girl.

Kathlyn in *Captain Kate,* 1911, one of the wild animal pictures with which she became identified.

Kathlyn-style coiffures and hats while the gents carried a postcard pose of their favorite film star.

With their anti-heroes and promiscuous heroines cavorting in and out of beds on the screen, today's generation has no concept of the tremendous influence a movie star had in the cinema's early days and in our "sophisticated" day and age, it's difficult to understand the impact which a particular film had on the general public, especially since Selig under-exploited his serial by economizing on release prints, covering the entire country with only 24.

The success of *The Adventures of Kathlyn* placed her in line for better and bigger stories; Kathlyn gave a distinguished performance as Cherry Molette in the screen's first version of Rex Beach's novel, *The Spoilers,* and followed this with a finely drawn characterization in *The Rosary.* With these and her role as Edith Courtland in another Beach hit, *The Ne'er-Do-Well* (a story of the Panama Canal), Miss Williams established herself as one of the outstanding dramatic heroines of the period.

Selig's studio closed its doors in 1918. While his pro-German attitudes were well-known at a time when public sympathy was swinging from neutralism to the British side, Selig's collapse was not caused by his political activities, as some writers have suggested. His papers and records are among the archives of the Academy of Motion Picture Arts and Sciences and establish a close relationship in the decline of his fortunes tied in with the decline suffered by the Motion Picture Patents Company and its General Film Company, which released much of the Selig product. Few of his special productions in 1916–17 received the widespread distribution which once automatically guaranteed a handsome profit, and costs were accelerating out of sight for the smaller producers. In addition, Kathlyn's reputation and popularity had rapidly grown beyond Selig's ability to afford her talent and the showman lost his star to Paramount in late 1916. This blow, along with the departure of Tom Santschi and other box-office attractions, hastened the inevitable closing of Selig's studio.

Kathlyn appeared in several of the Oliver Morosco pictures produced for Paramount release (*Redeeming Love, Out of the Wreck, Big Timber*), and by 1918 she had become one of Zukor's

With Harold Lockwood in *The Tide of Destiny*.

stellar attractions. But after her Paramount contract expired, Kathlyn turned to free-lancing, allowing her to spend more time as Mrs. Charles Eyton, the producer whom she married in 1916 (her first marriage to Victor Kainer had been dissolved). Free-lancing allowed her a wider choice in roles and she worked for many of the major producers in the next few years. Two films made with Roy Stewart as her male lead stand out among Miss Williams's performances of the period—Benjamin B. Hampton's production of Zane Grey's *The U.P. Trail* and Universal's *Trimmed in Scarlet.*

When her son (by Kainer) died in 1922, Miss Williams began to limit her appearances, gradually drifting into more mature and matronly roles. Approaching 40, she was still the handsome woman of twenty years earlier; not exactly what you'd call beautiful, but her carriage and bearing, including a habit of holding her head erect, created an air of self-assurance which gave Kathlyn an attention-holding profile, setting her apart instantly from the many new faces crowding the screen in the twenties.

Her popularity waned as the decade wore on, and although she tried the talkies Kathlyn decided that she and the movies had already given each other their best. After completing *Rendezvous At Midnight* for Universal in 1934, she retired to a quiet life in Hollywood, entertaining occasionally and traveling. Over the years, her fans lost track of their one-time favorite until 1949, when Kathlyn was returning from Las Vegas with a friend. Their car left the highway and plunged over an embankment. The accident cost Kathlyn one leg. News of her accident was carried by the wire services, resulting in a flood of letters from those who still remembered sharing her exciting adventures so many years before. Confined to a wheelchair, Kathlyn Williams finally died of a heart attack on September 24, 1960.

It's too bad that so many of the screen personalities passed away without leaving their memories and recollections on the printed page. The task of the film historians of the future would have been immeasurably lighter had such information been collected in a systematic manner by some recognized archival agency. Although the pioneer companies like Selig were important to the growth of the motion picture, insufficient first-hand information concerning the behind-the-scenes operation of the industry is available; The Selig Girl could have made a valuable contribution had she written her autobiography. As it stands, all the public has to remember her by are memories and a few of the many films she made.

Kathlyn's age was showing in *The World's Applause,* 1923, with Adolphe Menjou.

With Betty Compson, Theodore von Eltz, and Robert Edeson in *Locked Doors,* 1924.

CLARA KIMBALL YOUNG

One of the saddest stories told in Hollywood concerns the star who had an abundance of talent, yet received poor advice, suffered from bad management, undertook the wrong roles and refused to face reality, watching a carefully constructed career disappear from view without lifting a finger to prevent it. Repeated time after time with many variations over the years, the story is an old one, but every time I hear it, my memory softly backpedals a half-century to what must have been the original version, starring Clara Kimball Young.

When she turned 21 in 1912, Clara had everything working in her favor. The daughter of two reasonably prominent stage personalities (Edward Marshall Kimball and Pauline Madden), she had received her theatrical initiation at age three and over the years became an accomplished actress on her own. Married to actor James Young, Clara left a touring stock company in Salt Lake City to appear on the screen with Vitagraph. While New York City and the movies were a long way from her Benton Harbor, Michigan, birthplace, Clara's portrayals in *Ransomed, The Sepoy's Wife* and *Rock of Ages* launched a most promising career and the future looked even brighter.

At Vitagraph, James Young became a successful screen director and Clara played a variety of roles. With good material like *Cardinal Wolsey* and *My Official Wife,* she quickly acquired a box-office following. Although excelling at dramatic fare, she might as easily have become a fine comedienne. Before teaming with his wife,

CLARA KIMBALL YOUNG

Sidney Drew appeared with Miss Young in several Vitagraph comedies like *Goodness Gracious* and the popular comic had the highest regard for her talent and sense of comic timing. But Clara had other ambitions which surfaced when she left Vitagraph for the World Film Corporation in 1915.

***The Little Minister*, 1913.**

Within three years, her paycheck read $1000 every week, and although Vitagraph felt she was worth more they declined to pay it because of her husband's pride. Each time they raised her salary, they were forced by good taste to raise his in order to avoid a domestic tangle which would have spilled over into their professional lives. Enter Lewis J. Selznick, a resourceful newcomer to the business with great plans and a gift of gab. Selznick and Clara quickly became good friends, especially after he announced that she would figure heavily in his plans for his forthcoming production company. Walking away with Vitagraph's star attraction, Selznick used her prestigious name and his own persuasive talents in selling stock to finance his venture. Pouring the money into Clara's features, he paid handsome dividends to each investor with the receipts. All went well for awhile, but Selznick was eventually maneuvered out of World by his own partners. Taking Clara with him, he formed the million dollar Clara Kimball Young Film Corporation with a personal investment of only $1000.

As Clara's pictures had done a very large portion of World's business, her departure was a body blow to the company and William A. Brady was unable to salvage the remains; Selznick prospered while World died. The producer had become such a charming addition to Clara's entourage that in 1916, her husband sued for divorce, naming Selznick as a correspondent. Undisturbed by the whole affair, Clara later complained to interviewers that while she had always been dependent upon the advice of men, she had been unlucky in love. Proposals poured in weekly from her admirers and one gentleman reputedly offered her a million dollars if she would marry him. But standing at the pinnacle of her career, Clara reserved the right to choose her own companions and her next heart-throb proved to be her undoing. Harry Garson took over as Clara's manager, director, confidante and resident Wizard of Oz, in spite of protests from her friends that he would bring her only grief. By 1923, the Clara Kimball Young Film Corporation had been dissolved, Clara was bankrupt and no producer in town would touch her as long as there was a possibility that hiring her meant having Garson on their set.

The Flat Above.

Clara, when she formed her own company.

The Woman of Bronze, 1923.

Goodness Gracious or *Movies As They Shouldn't Be,* a 1914 Vitagraph spoof of melodramatic movies with Clara, Sidney Drew, and Ned Finlay.

The Interrupted Honeymoon.

Clara's downfall actually resulted from a combination of circumstances. Her girlish beauty of Vitagraph days was gone, replaced by a more mature appearance. The sure directorial touch of her former husband was lacking and once Garson assumed control of her career Clara's popularity began to sag. At World in 1915–16, she had progressed from the light-hearted *Marrying Money* and *Heart of The Blue Ridge* to deep emotional drama in *Camille* (a very good film at the time) and *The Yellow Passport.* Miss Young's later films for her own company, released through Selznick and then Equity, were strongly emotional, almost melodramatic in nature and suffered from complex scripts and Garson's uneven direction. Clara sometimes attempted too much, as in *The Worldly Madonna,* which saw her in a dual role as Sister and Sinner. Her characterization of the nun was too pious to undergo so radical a change demanded by the script and the cabaret singer was etched too deeply with sin to impersonate a nun successfully—Clara simply failed to carry the audience with her.

Interestingly enough, her closest competitor in the deeply emotional waters in which she chose to work was Pauline Frederick,

***The Foolish Virgin,* 1917.**

whose career climaxed at just about the same time and bore striking similarities along the way. As Clara's films became more and more sophisticated and stylized, her appeal narrowed to female fans and release of her pictures became more difficult to arrange, earning less at the box-office. It was a chain reaction of circumstances which forced Clara into a premature retirement, and although she attempted to return to the screen her efforts to regain her wealth and fame were less than successful. Clara pawned her jewelry collection in the twenties, tried a comeback in 1931 and auctioned her possessions in 1932, working occasionally in minor roles during the thirties. In 1940, her appearance in *The Roundup* was heralded as a new comeback, but it was only a press agent's dream.

Although a steady, dependable performer in the last years of her stardom, the level of mediocrity with which Garson surrounded Clara was more than even her talent could overcome. Yet the lady never had an unkind word to offer about him in public and refused all consideration of letting Garson fend for himself. Adolph Zukor

As Anne Boleyn in *Cardinal Wolsey,* 1912. Tefft Johnson portrayed Henry VIII.

once offered Clara $7000 weekly and 25 percent of the profits, but stipulated that Garson could not set foot on the set. She passed away in 1960, a forgotten woman by all but serious movie buffs, some of whom recalled her days of glory. Most knew her only as the star of *Eyes of Youth,* periodically revived at the Silent Movie Theater in Hollywood.